THE FILMS OF FRED SCHEPISI

THE FILMS OF FRED SCHEPISI

Brian McFarlane

University Press of Mississippi / Jackson

The University Press of Mississippi is the scholarly publishing agency of the Mississippi Institutions of Higher Learning: Alcorn State University, Delta State University, Jackson State University, Mississippi State University, Mississippi University for Women, Mississippi Valley State University, University of Mississippi, and University of Southern Mississippi.

www.upress.state.ms.us

The University Press of Mississippi is a member of the Association of University Presses.

Copyright © 2022 by University Press of Mississippi
All rights reserved
Manufactured in the United States of America

First printing 2022

∞

Library of Congress Control Number: 2021042953
Hardback ISBN 978-1-4968-3535-2
Trade paperback ISBN 978-1-4968-3530-7
Epub single ISBN 978-1-4968-3534-5
Epub institutional ISBN 978-1-4968-3533-8
PDF single ISBN 978-1-4968-3532-1
PDF institutional ISBN 978-1-4968-3531-4
British Library Cataloging-in-Publication Data available

CONTENTS

Acknowledgments vii
Preface. ix
Chapter One: Early Days 3
Chapter Two: Emerging Filmmaker 10
Chapter Three: A "Master-Work"—*The Chant of Jimmie Blacksmith*. 28
Chapter Four: Making It Overseas 42
Chapter Five: Schepisi and the Chamberlain Affair—*A Cry in the Dark*. 66
Chapter Six: At Home in the US 77
Chapter Seven: Triumph in the UK—*Last Orders* (2002) 97
Chapter Eight: In the New Century 112
Chapter Nine: At Home and Abroad. 131
Conclusion 146
Filmography 151
Notes 161
Select Bibliography. 173
Index 175

ACKNOWLEDGMENTS

Among the many to whom I am grateful for their support for this project, first of all I thank the University Press of Mississippi for providing such positive and helpful responses to the original proposal and to subsequent queries.

I am indebted to Fred Schepisi for the interview time he gave me on several occasions, and to several of his colleagues who provided valuable insights into his working procedures. These include Ian Baker, Jill Bilccock, Helen Morse, and Brian Tufano, and to novelist Tom Keneally, who was variously associated with Fred's first three films. Thanks are also due to Tom Ryan, for his book of interviews with Fred and for the long-term loan of DVD versions of many of the director's films.

There was also a great deal of help from the staffs of the Australian Film Institute's Research Library, Melbourne, from the British Film Institute Library, London, from the Australian Centre of the Moving Image, Melbourne, and the National Film and Sound Archive, Melbourne. I greatly valued the generous time the staff of each of these institutions gave me in necessary and diverse processes, whether in locating obscure early short films by Schepisi or making available masses of useful published material.

My grateful thanks are due to Peter Tapp, managing editor of *Metro*, Melbourne, to Matthew Frost, the head of editorial at Manchester University Press, publisher of my book *Twenty British Films: A Guided Tour*, and Mark Freeman, coeditor of the online journal *Senses of Cinema*, for permission to draw substantially on my article on *The Devil's Playground*, my chapter on *Last Orders*, and my review of *The Eye of the Storm*.

Finally, I thank the Centre for Urban Transitions at Swinburne University of Technology, Melbourne, for providing me with such a congenial writing space, and as always I am very grateful to my daughter Sophie for formatting and tidying up my manuscript.

PREFACE

Over the last few decades, I found that I had written several times about individual films directed by Fred Schepisi, often several years apart, without ever having to arrive at any comprehensive account of his achievement as a filmmaker. It was when I was doing the research for a study of his first major feature, *The Devil's Playground* (1976), for an article in 2014 in the Melbourne journal *Metro*, that it occurred to me that it was time for an overall investigation of his work in three continents. There have been plenty of articles, many of which I shall draw on, about this or that film, and interviews with him about these, but not yet a full-length study of his emergence as an Australian *and* international filmmaker.

Whether this would reveal ongoing continuities in his preoccupations or stylistic traits I couldn't be sure from the freestanding pieces I'd written in various publications. The first of these earlier studies was in a long-ish review of *The Chant of Jimmie Blacksmith* in a 1978 issue of the journal *Cinema Papers* and subsequently a chapter on this in my 1983 book, *Words and Images: Australian Novels into Film*. These were followed by another quite long review of *Six Degrees of Separation* in a 1995 issue of *Cinema Papers*, a review of *The Eye of the Storm* for the online journal *Senses of Cinema* (2011), the 2014 article on *The Devil's Playground* in *Metro*, and a chapter on *Last Orders* in my 2015 book, *Twenty British Films: A Guided Tour*. I'd also done a public lecture on *Plenty* in 1987. What would a comprehensive exploration of these and his other dozen films, mostly made in the US, with the odd return to Australia or sortie to the UK, reveal about his status as an international director? My chapter headings, while not wildly original, aim to encapsulate his mobility.

Curiosity about this and other matters relating to Schepisi's output, spurred on by a very lively and thoughtful interview he gave me in connection with my essay on *The Devil's Playground*, led me to plan the present volume. Further interview time with him confirmed my sense that he was a filmmaker with a notably perceptive approach to his art—and, indeed, to its business aspects, without serious attention to which films might not get made. It seemed to me that a comprehensive study of his oeuvre was long overdue, for his place as an Australian director who had acquired an international reputation for a striking filmography and who had command of film as both art form and commercial enterprise.

Essentially this book traces a career through its chronological sequence, but it also seeks to consider, as each film is thus explored, such elements as seem to suggest parallels—stylistic and thematic—elsewhere in his films, or that appear to offer the director new challenges, or both. Above all, this study is concerned with exploring the kind of filmmaker who emerges from a wide-ranging filmography. I shall argue that while Schepisi works in many diverse genres he never seems constrained by their conventions, that there is a clear sense of how he, in narrative and visual aspects for instance, stamps his films with a memorable individuality.

As will become apparent in this study, there are some key recurring elements in his films, wherever they were made and whatever their genres. For instance, he was always interested in the interaction of individuals and communities, believing that perhaps this "accounts for why many of [his] films are ensemble films as opposed to single-star vehicles";[1] he had an ongoing approach to the adaptation of other media to film and strong views on this matter; and the visual qualities of his films are always a key guide to their intellectual and emotional content. While there are a couple of films with which he was not wholly satisfied, to speak of "a Schepisi film" does resonate persuasively. This is not just to invoke the term "auteur," which implies that the film is above all the product of the director's vision. For him, as will become apparent, film is essentially a collaborative enterprise, and he was a director who acquired—and valued—associates who found him amenable to suggestion and who enabled him to achieve his aims.

In pursuing so many aspects of Schepisi's approach to the making of his films and to the processes of filmmaking at large, I have found Tom Ryan's edited collection *Fred Schepisi: Interviews* (2017) to be invaluable. Schepisi emerges through its dozens of discussions as a director with some clear ideas about what he wants his films to say—and how he goes about ensuring that they do so.

THE FILMS OF FRED SCHEPISI

Chapter One

EARLY DAYS

In the 1970s, Australian cinema saw a revival of interest—the term "renaissance" was even sometimes invoked—such as it had not enjoyed for several decades, probably *never* if one considers the level of international acclaim it elicited. The reasons for this upsurge in the local product are complex, but one of the factors that now stands out is the emergence of a batch of directors who would not only make a significant contribution to the revival here but would also go on to success in the US or the UK or both. Such potent names include Peter Weir, Gillian Armstrong, Bruce Beresford—and Fred Schepisi. Schepisi's career trajectory is both typical of these key figures and perhaps the one that has achieved most wide-ranging success in three continents.

It is not the aim of the present study to provide a detailed biography of Schepisi, but two crucial factors of his early life and career would prove important in, at least partly, accounting for what followed. Born Frederic Alan Schepisi, in the Melbourne suburb of Richmond on December 26, 1939, he was educated at Assumption College, Kilmore, a Catholic boarding school, and subsequently at the Marist Brothers' Juniorate, Macedon, both in country Victoria.[1] The latter was for the training of those with a priestly vocation in mind. He was here from the age of thirteen, at his own suggestion, until he left school for good two years later, recalling, "by which time I had got it out of my system."[2] After finishing his education, he spent nearly two decades as a television production manager. The former of these two factors would influence ideologically his entry into feature film production, notably with *The Devil's Playground* (1976), which drew on his educational experiences and religious background. The second is important in understanding how he acquired the commercial know-how that he would bring to bear on the world of feature film production, as well as the artistic kudos that came with winning awards for some of the short films he made at this time.

Perhaps, too, I should add a third recurring characteristic of the key 1970s films of Schepisi and of those other directors mentioned above. They all made memorable movies that focused on rites of passage and had a coming-of-age theme: Weir's *Picnic at Hanging Rock* (1975), Schepisi's *The Devil's Playground* (1976), Beresford's *The Getting of Wisdom* (1977), and Armstrong's *My Brilliant Career* (1979). Could this have something to do with the idea of a burgeoning film industry or, even more basically, with the notion of Australia's assuming a more sophisticated approach to national identity, its rite of passage involving a loosening of ties with the "mother country," as Britain used to be referred to, following the election of Gough Whitlam's Labor Government in 1972? However, as Australian writer Sue Matthews warns: "The 1972 election of the reforming Labor government did not automatically transform Australia into an independent filmmaker's paradise."[3] Maybe not, but it does seem that there was a freer approach to Australian culture that the change of government encouraged.

Born in Richmond, Schepisi lived first in the up-market suburb of Toorak, where his father ran a fruit shop. He subsequently moved to an eastern suburb, Balwyn, where his father had a used-car sale yard, and he and his wife, Mary, at present (2019) have an apartment on the thirty-seventh floor of Melbourne's tallest building, the Eureka Tower. In between was a spell in the beach-side suburb of Albert Park. The point of listing some of his residences is to suggest that, whatever successes he has experienced overseas, his identity as an Australian—and specifically Melbournian—has always been a crucial factor in his career, however successfully he has adapted to production processes in other countries. Like those other directors of the "revival," he has made significant filmmaking returns to his home country.

GETTING STARTED

Out of school at fifteen, Schepisi started in advertising as a dispatch boy and went into the press production department when television came to Melbourne in 1956, the year in which the city was hosting the Olympic Games. He recalls: "By the end of that year [1956], I found myself doing a lot of television commercials. They made me the head of Carden Advertising in Melbourne. Many of the people I was working with in the film companies had very little experience, so we were all doing it together."[4] No doubt, as Sue Matthews wrote: "Working in advertising allowed him to develop business skills as well as filmmaking ones,"[5] and these would stand him in good stead in the very different production climates of Australia and the US. The former could often be very difficult in the financing and distribution processes, whereas he found the US both more sophisticated and more demandingly complex. It was also at this time that he became fascinated by the foreign—or as they used to be called, "continental"— films he saw, and which would later become influential on his filmmaking practice. With the emergence of television in Australia, he began writing and producing as he worked on TV commercials, for which he won a number of awards.

After leaving Carden's, he and his friend Philip Adams, who became a very well-known figure in Australian broadcasting, moved to the Melbourne-based Paton Advertising Service, where Schepisi was television production manager and Adams was creative director. Three years later, as he recalled, he applied for and got a job with the former production studio Cinesound, in Melbourne. When he saw a job advertised with Cinesound, he recalls: "I put up my age about four years and got it. Over about eighteen months, a couple of friends of mine, Alex Stitt and Bruce Weatherhead, designers, were working with me; they weren't in the company but were writing ads and I was sending work to them and they to me . . . it was all commercials and documentaries."[6]

At Cinesound, where he was writing, producing, and directing, he eventually became its manager, and after running Cinesound for two years he bought it, and set up his own company, The Film House, of which he was managing director. Here, he had plenty of opportunity to exercise and extend his financial expertise *and* to get on with the business of filmmaking, which was what he was yearning to do. He acknowledged the value of this experience, saying: "Having a company helped me when I went into making features, knowing how to get the wherewithal to get the features off the ground and to invest in them as well."[7]

Among the short films Schepisi made in the 1960s and early '70s, four have been available for viewing, along with clips from a fifth. If the early short films are no longer widely known on their own merits, they *are* interesting for the ways in which they hint at the feature filmmaker who would become a key figure in the local scene in the ensuing decades.

The Shape of Quality (1965)

It is not necessary to have a passionate interest in the once-popular Volkswagen Beetle to find some stylish merit in *The Shape of Quality*, the twenty-seven-minute documentary directed by Schepisi at Cinesound for the Public Relations Department of Volkswagen Australia in 1965. A car races behind the title to some jaunty music (by B. Clarke and F. Smith; all credits are given with initial only for first names), and an off-screen narrator (J. Royle) takes over to announce the project and the car's virtues. It "seeks perfection through inspection," and the rest of the film makes much of the endless processes that go towards the moment when the completed car is driven off the assembly line, to the testing area, and then into the world at large.

Abetted by the editing of B(rian) Kavanagh, who would become one of his frequent collaborators, Schepisi manages to infuse the processes with some sense of drama, moving between long shots of the car body's descending to join up with the chassis or close-ups of screwing bolts or even of the logo—and intermittently shots of completed cars careering through rough waters. Though there is no sense of characterization, nor would one expect it, there are wide shots that place the human contribution in relation to the appearance of the final product (e.g., a Volkswagen Beetle), and its final inclusion in the scene of a family picnic. Placement of people in significant relation to their settings and their occupations would become a recurring aspect of Schepisi's feature films.

People Make Papers (1965)

This eighteen-minute documentary was produced by Cinesound for the Victorian newspaper *The Age*. Schepisi claimed that he was influenced by some notable documentary filmmakers in England, whose work in the 1950s, including Lindsay Anderson's *Every Day Except Christmas*, was shot by the great cameraman Walter Lassally.[8] This film draws on the work processes involved in the daily setting up of Covent Garden market, and one can see how its dealings with work schedules may have echoed for Schepisi in the making of *People Make Papers* in rendering the complex activities involved. Viewed over fifty years later, it now offers a fascinating historical account of how a daily newspaper was put together: the sources of the news; the reporters on the spot, then in their offices madly typing away at their stories; telephone operators receiving reports; the printers going to work setting up the typeface in the small hours, galley proofs pinned around the walls; and the papers finally pouring off the printing presses prior to being distributed all over the city.

Schepisi puts these processes before us in a lively montage of some of the news items, including riots in the American south, a robbery in the posh Melbourne suburb Toorak, a footballer being massaged, more riots, this time in Trafalgar Square, the queen returning to official duties after a minor indisposition, and so on. The value of this short film, which won an Australian Film Institute Award, is not so much in the recalling of these long-ago events as in the record it provides of what a massive and frantic business the production of a major newspaper was in the days of cumbersome machinery and the absence of computers. The last moments of the film cut from the delivery of vast bundles of the paper to the now-empty office and the still production room. In the limited running time, Schepisi, with his then-regular editor, Kavanagh, creates an eloquent contrast between the actual events and the frenzied work involved in bringing them to the paper's readers, the pounding noise of the presses contrasted with the almost ghostly quiet of the last minutes.

A Hundred-Odd Years from Now (1968)

Made for The Film House was a somewhat bizarre commercial called *A Hundred-Odd Years from Now*. Viewing this without preceding knowledge, I felt in its opening minutes that it was going to be some kind of feminist tract, full of images of women, with expressionless faces and slim upright figures, in strange leotard-type outfits, standing in front of various machines. With no man in sight, and a poster proclaiming "FORGET MEN," as well as the announcement "WOMEN RUN THINGS" on their backs, this was an easy mistake for the viewer to make. Then, curiously, the seventeen-minute film cuts to a forest, with men walking through, and a voice-over that proves to belong to a handsome, apparently adventuresome young guy called Yockoo, who appears quite pleased with himself. The voice-over tells us, "I'm off to find the city," and lists all the appliances and institutions he hopes to find there.

When he fetches up at the women's workplace, he recites this list in full; they surround him and put a sort of electronic helmet over his head. Before they go to work on him, there is an insert of his home town Mildura, Victoria, with glimpses of his mother and his girlfriend—and of the grape-picking industry. This latter is our first intimation of what this commercial short is at heart about: the endless digestive value of dried fruit. Schepisi later aptly described it as "a crazy futuristic thing about an all-female world and a man whom they stumble across, take as a prisoner and show how good dried fruits can be."[9] "Crazy," perhaps, but also inventive in the way it makes its points with wit and visual acuity.

Tomorrow's Canberra (1972)

Made for the Australian Commonwealth Film Unit, this thirty-four-minute documentary was set up by the National Capital Development Commission. The brief of the latter, inaugurated in 1957, was to plan, develop, and construct the National Capital: that is, to provide for "Tomorrow's Canberra." Written and directed by Schepisi, it opens with a series of titles, each preceded by a date, recording the history of Canberra, from 1900 when, in the wake of Federation, the constitution required the establishment of a national capital. The American architect Walter Burley Griffin won first prize in the competition for the design of the new capital. These titles lead up to the 1927 opening of the Parliament House and, proleptically, to 2000, "Tomorrow's Canberra."

After this rather prosaic introduction, a voice-over is heard over a long shot of seven men sitting at a planning table, interspersed with shots of the opening of Parliament and of the building inside and out. There is some imaginative visual effect in the montage of images of the building, of World War I, of the Australian War Memorial, with serene vistas of the natural environment and images of construction. These images are intercut with episodes in which the planners consider such matters as the convenience of those living there, to promote a development that may enable the growth of a community spirit. Shots of people playing sports or singing, of people in relation to the environment, both natural and structured, may in hindsight seem to anticipate Schepisi's ongoing concern for the interaction of people and setting in his feature film career.

In this short film, he manages to infuse some sense of drama into the planning activities and to give point to the film's final remark: "A national capital is only built once in a nation's history." It's not just about chaps expressing their views in a planning room: Schepisi, with his longtime cinematographer Ian Baker, reminds us that, much as buildings matter, there are wider societal issues at stake.

...

Schepisi directed and wrote hundreds of advertisements and documentaries for The Film House,[10] of which the above are some of the more substantial survivors. The fifth from which brief clips only survive, *Onward Speed* (1971), depicts two people with a small replica of an Australian postal pillar-box from which they magically extract letters, ending up with a coffin full of them! As for the other short films discussed above, at their best, they evince an imagination's engaging with what might have been didactic purposes. There were also a couple of long-forgotten short films, *Party* (1970) and *Can't You Hear Me Callin', Caroline* (1971), before Schepisi's first serious grappling with the drama of human conflicts in *The Priest*, his contribution to a portmanteau film, *Libido* (1973). There had been enough—and diverse—signs of engagement with film's narrative and visual potential, as well as with the commercial rigors involved, to find him well prepared for what followed. He had also established a valuable talent for working productively with others who would become key collaborators when he turned to feature filmmaking.

Chapter Two

EMERGING FILMMAKER

The 1973 portmanteau film *Libido* was Schepisi's entry into commercial filmmaking after nearly a decade of industrial documentaries and short films, of the kind discussed in the preceding chapter. Schepisi directed *The Priest*, the third of the quartet of films that comprised *Libido*. If the film is not much heard of now, it was undoubtedly significant in several contemporary contexts, such as those of its production history and thematic concerns.

PRODUCTION SCENE

As with much Australian filmmaking at this time, the financing of *Libido* was no easy matter. The four short films that made up the feature were all shot in and around Melbourne, with an overall budget of A$120,000, "backed by A$25,000 from the Australian Council of the Arts and approximately A$15,000 from members of the Victorian branch of the Producers and Directors Guild of Australia [PDGA]."[1] Schepisi paid for his portion of the film from his own resources, but, after some inevitably difficult financing problems, the film was acquired by British Empire Film (BEF) Distributors, which "also funded the blow-up from 16mm to 35mm"[2] and publicized it vigorously. It opened at Melbourne's Rapallo Theatre on April 6, 1973, and enjoyed a commercially lively season of three months.

The authors of one key reference on Australian film wrote: "The film was derived from a series of workshops conducted in 1971 by the Producers and Directors Guild of Australia . . . to acquaint writers with the needs of narrative film."[3] So, the guild was the key element both in the economics of the film's production and in how it came to be, in formal and thematic terms. John B. Murray, the president of the Victorian branch of the PDGA and director of one of the *Libido* quartet, was interested in encouraging authors associated with other media to turn their attention to screenwriting. The four writers finally selected were playwright David Williamson, cultural historian Craig McGregor, memoirist/novelist Hal Porter, and novelist Thomas Keneally, the latter the author of Schepisi's screenplay. All had been invited, along with other writers, to prepare short stories based on the theme of love in its infinite variety. As Keneally remembered: "Fred was impressed with the talents that had gone into making industrials and documentaries, and now he wanted to dedicate these to making feature films."[4]

THE TRENDY '70s

That brief phrase, "the theme of love," hardly does justice to what was going on in society—and in Australian film—during the early 1970s. There was an outspokenness about matters of sexuality and gender that is reflected in the films that were being made in Australia (and, indeed, elsewhere in the world), in the wake, no doubt, of the culturally revolutionary decade that preceded the Australian film revival. Women were dispensing with bras, Gay Lib was attracting large demonstrations, nudity no longer seemed outrageous, and feminism's voice was making itself heard in the cause of women's empowerment. As Meaghan Morris wrote, "The revival of the Australian film industry has coincided with a period in which traditional views of the family, love, sexual norms and male-female relationships have come under attack in all western, industrialized countries."[5]

I don't mean that these motifs or themes were necessarily spelled out didactically in the Australian film scene, but the kinds of film that provided the cinematic context for *Libido* could often be described, in the terms of one commentator, who wrote: "Parallel with the sex comedy was another energetic strain of comedy films . . . [that] have since come to be known as the 'ocker' comedies."[6] In this respect, titles that come to mind include *Jack and Jill: A Postscript* (1970), *The Naked Bunyip* (1970), *Stork* (1971), *The Adventures of Barry McKenzie* (1972), and *Alvin Purple* (1973). These and others later in the decade each tackled sexual matters with varying degrees of seriousness, most often for comedy, and were among the most commercially successful films of the decade in Australia. As one author wrote of *Libido* and those other films named above: "Key productions [such as these] made use of recently liberalized attitudes to on-screen sex and violence to build an awareness of the visibility of Australian films."[7] There was obviously a new frankness in the air, whether in the specifically "sex comedies" or in those exploiting the "ocker"[8] image of the randy male.

Libido (1973)

There are clearly elements of both these generic trends in the *Libido* quartet, but Schepisi's twenty-eight-minute contribution, *The Priest*, "concern[ing] the unconsummatable infatuation of a nun and a priest for each other"[9] dealt with sexual impulses in much more obviously serious mode. Nevertheless, intertextual references and aspects of cultural change are always worth considering in relation to any given film text, and *Libido* is clearly not an exception to this. The other three films in the quartet bear this out in their different ways: in John B. Murray's *The Husband*, the wife's dominance leads the husband to fantasize about sex orgies; in Tim Burstall's *The Child*, the youthful protagonist is shocked when he sees the governess he adores making love to a local playboy; *The Priest* is third in the quartet; and in the final film, ironically entitled *The Family Man*, both the sex- and ocker-comedy strains come into play when a couple of boozy guys fail to have their way with the women they have picked up in a bar. The whole film offers a series of reflections on the sort of freedom in such matters that was, by 1973, very much a part of the new Australian film scene.

In his essay "The Guild—A Brief History," which accompanied the DVD release of *Libido*, John Murray wrote: "In 1969, sex—or in the case of *Libido*, the sex-drive—was not a subject openly discussed in our quite relaxed yet somewhat repressed society. Our heads had become divorced from our genitals and we felt that this gulf needed to be bridged. As there also appeared a growing desire in the community to do so, the Guild in Victoria resolved to pursue the topic in our workshop productions."[10] By 1973, there was more open discussion of sexual matters than Murray noted in 1969, and Schepisi, working from Thomas Keneally's screenplay, directly addresses the painful conflict between religious belief and carnal urge, with an openness that might not have been likely in preceding decades.

So, there is a complex ethical context in which to situate any consideration of Schepisi's first venture into feature film.

The Priest

By the time Schepisi began shooting his segment of *Libido*, he had—as discussed in chapter one—plenty of experience in the techniques of filmmaking, whether in his highly successful commercials for his own company, Film House, or in the short films he made with staff and students at Swinburne College of Technology. And, embarking on *The Priest*, he had the advantage of working with several collaborators from those earlier ventures. These included such key personnel as cinematographer Ian Baker, music composer Bruce Smeaton, and editor Brian Kavanagh, with all of whom he would work again (as he would with stars Arthur Dignam and Robyn Nevin). No doubt, the presence of colleagues whose value he knew contributed to the confidence with which he approached this new phase of his career.

In an interview he gave as one of the DVD special features, Schepisi spoke about how the original screenplay for *The Priest* was overwritten because it had been intended for stage and TV. Seeing the novelist Keneally's name among those whose attention the PDGA was interested in attracting, Schepisi asked him to pare back the script, so that there was "about one-third less dialogue when we started shooting."[11]

An ex-seminarian, Keneally said: "It was the religious theme that drew me to working on *The Priest*. I was interested at the time in the issue of celibacy, which I thought would end, and in the longueurs of priests and nuns who were falling for each other, and renouncing their vows but always with great angst of course."[12] The film is essentially a two-hander in which a priest and a nun are for almost the length of the film confined to a single room of the religious house in which Sister Caroline (Nevin) practices her vocation. In the opening shot, the priest, Father Burns (Dignam), arrives at the grand-looking mansion and asks to see Caroline, who has not wanted them to meet "secretly," says the elderly nun (Vivean Gray) who admits him, adding, "I respect her for that." This brief exchange alerts us to the conflict within each of—and perhaps between—Caroline and Burns, and at least to her wish for there being nothing furtive about whatever is between them.

Schepisi was in no doubt about what constituted the core of his film. What really mattered to him, he recalls in the DVD interview, "is what's happening between these two people," and in Dignam and Nevin he had two actors more than equal to the task. His then-wife Rhonda Finlayson served as the casting director on the film, and Schepisi valued her teaching him not to look for "types" but to remember that actors can be chameleons.[13] It is no exaggeration to say that in Dignam and Nevin he had found such performers who seem wholly absorbed in their respective characters. Schepisi in another interview said of these two: "They had never acted in a film before, and so were very interested in the process. They were a great help to me."[14]

The notion of a priest and a nun in love was—and probably still is—controversial material for a film, especially when, in brief flashback (or fantasy moment?), they are seen in naked coitus. Burns is prepared to sever his ties with the Vatican to marry Caroline. He tells her that "the Pope has no more authority than Chairman Mao to tell me I can't marry," and, following an inserted shot of his ordination, he asserts: "I've grown out of the priest I became in 1963." For Caroline, it is less clear-cut: "I have to be able to marry within the Church eventually. I couldn't *live* with you. I must be able to marry you as a Catholic." Whereas she can say with conviction: "I won't act against principle for anyone," Burns can only attest: "All I believe in is you." As Meaghan Morris noted: "The priest argues that the nun cares more for dogma or opinion than she does for him; the nun argues that he is trying to destroy the innocence for which he loved her in the first place."[15]

Their encounter, with brief inserts of life beyond this room, ends with her telling him to "ask me again . . . when I'm free to go," as he strides out of the building. The last shot of each shows her crouched over with grief in the room, as though she is still bound by its walls, and him equally wracked on a bench in the garden. After the aforementioned cuts, Schepisi is left with dialogue of an intelligence and intensity that works persuasively with Baker's camerawork to create a moving sense of the struggle that informs the film: that is, a sharp and painful treatment of the tension that dogma can create in relation to sexual urgings.

In the DVD interview, Schepisi recalled feeling that the film was originally "too techniquy," having believed that, if your film was largely a matter of two people talking in a room, "you had to lighten it up," but that this didn't mean that "you [had] to jazz it up visually." He and Baker then tried different approaches to lighting, and, influenced by the French New Wave, they decided to make more use of natural lighting. The resulting effect is a kind of quiet realism that ensures that the emphasis remains where Schepisi wanted it to be: on the two protagonists. This is a film about a critical moment in the lives of these two people, and the camera knows when to focus on one while the lighting on the other is more subdued, or when both faces in close-up enact the tension between them. He also spoke about the close-up in which the process of pouring and handing on cups of tea is not just an arbitrary cutaway from the actors' faces, but a detail that records the politeness of the world they live in—and why they are as they are.

The film trusts its two chief actors to embody the conflicting issues that are making their lives a matter of anguish at this point. The drama is in the way they look and stand, whether looking at or away from each other. Apparently Nevin wore no makeup because Schepisi was aiming for a realistic effect and he received some criticism for this.[16] He wanted to echo the truth that nuns did not use makeup. A recent re-viewing of the 1945 Hollywood film *The Bells of St Mary's* convinces me that Schepisi was right in such a decision: Nevin looks a far more convincing nun than the carefully cosmeticized Sister Ingrid Bergman in the earlier film.

What we are left with after a viewing of this short film is the sense of a director who trusts his actors to incarnate the central conflict—of the role of the erotic, which can be at such painful odds with the individual as a whole person, of its potential for shattering a sense of balanced wholeness. The nun and the priest are in love with each other, but they differ in the degrees to which their spiritual commitments will come between them and the consummation of their passion. In its dealings with this conflict, *The Priest* anticipates some of the concerns of his next film, *The Devil's Playground*, which draws on aspects of Schepisi's own Catholic background.

Libido Screened

The film received limited release in Australia through the Greater Union Organisation's chain of cinemas, opening, as noted above, at the Rapallo Theatre, Melbourne, where it ran for a strong three-month season.[17] Though it may have suggested a prurient interest in sexual matters, it was essentially "art-house" fare, and seems not to have been much distributed overseas. In London and in Spain, Schepisi's contribution to the portmanteau had to be deleted on grounds of its inherently controversial material.

Although *Libido* apparently failed to recoup half of its budget at the box office, whereas the likes of such contemporary Australian films as *Barry McKenzie* and *Alvin Purple* showed a profit of greater than 100 percent of their production costs,[18] its critical reception was more heartening, and its reputation has fared well in subsequent writings. Two contrary responses in the same journal, *Nation Review*, suggest that it wasn't going to be an unequivocal hit. Max Thomas claimed that it showed "eight leading Australian talents scrambling onto the sex bandwagon in an orgy of self-indulgence," while Bob Ellis reported that he felt "for the first time completely relaxed into the idea that the Australian film business was here to stay."[19]

Sandra Hall, writing at the time, noted the film's "stylised treatment of shadowed lighting and almost balletic camera movements," adding that "Schepisi and his crew have put as much movement as possible into the Keneally script, *The Priest*" and that "it remains the most static of the stories—acerbic but tortuous, effective mainly because of Arthur Dignam."[20] The term "static" probably derives from the film's limited setting and focus on two characters, but the shrewd use of camera and the cutting back of the dialogue referred to above ensure that the "action" remains focused on its key location: the faces of the protagonists. A later critical commentary describes *The Priest* as the most "intellectual" of the four films, "in the sense that it takes the form of an argument about the issue of sexual passion and purity of motive in the face of Catholic celibacy.... [The film's central] encounter occurs in a single closed room and acquires a chamber-theatre intensity as the camera circles and enacts their entrapment by their religious vows."[21] Decades later, that seems an insightful summation of the film's thematic and visual impact.

The Devil's Playground (1976)

The film that made Schepisi a name to reckon with in the Australian film revival of the 1970s was one which drew strongly on the recollections of his own early schooldays, spent (as referred to in chapter one) in a Catholic boarding school and subsequently a Marist Brothers Juniorate, both in country Victoria. When I asked him if he would describe the main source of *The Devil's Playground* as semi-autobiographical, he replied:

> Yes, absolutely. Probably a lot more than *semi*-autobiographical. I was wondering what would be a good idea for a film, and I thought, well, what I experienced was something a lot of people didn't. And one of my philosophies is that, within every walk of life, you always have the full range of personalities, whether it's architecture or plumbers or construction workers, you'll find the optimist, the pessimist, the bright one, the dull one, and in the monastery, among all the brothers, you'd find the same range of personalities. So that was the starting point: the exploring of different attitudes and the ways people look at things in the same environment. Also, what those brothers represent could be what any one of those young boys was likely to become, depending on, in the first place, their basic personalities and the influences they're exposed to.[22]

There is of course a good deal more to the film than recollections of his own education, but, as one account notes, though it shares the coming-of-age concerns of some of the major period films of the Australian revival, "it doesn't qualify for costume-drama lyricism and it is semi-autobiographical rather than literary in origin."[23] Further, as another critic wrote of several such key films of the period, including *The Devil's Playground* and Schepisi's subsequent effort, *The Chant of Jimmie Blacksmith*, rather than "plotted melodrama," "they were character, not action-based narratives with a past setting."[24]

However, to the extent that he was educated in a monastery from the age of thirteen, at his own suggestion, till he left school for good two years later, "by which time I had got it out of my system,"[25] as he said, the film has some roots in his life. His attitude to this stage of his life is important in relation to the film's pervading tone and attitudes, as will be explored later. On a more prosaic but no less important level, what happened in his life after leaving the Catholic boarding school (a "juniorate") for the training of those with a priestly vocation eventually propelled him into the business of filmmaking, as discussed in chapter one.

The company he bought, with its name changed to The Film House, became the production base for *The Devil's Playground*. Several decades later, he recalled some of the problems in setting up the film:

> It took five years to get it together and there was considerable resistance to it. The money was mostly from myself and friends and relatives, and some from the AFC [Australian Film Commission]. It wasn't till someone said I wasn't going to get any money from the government unless I was prepared to play tough and play politics, so I got tough and I played politics, because at that time I'd won more awards than anybody in Australia and internationally for my commercials, and for my documentaries, and I'd done a couple of short films, and part of the portmanteau film *Libido*.[26]

A more positive aspect of the film's production history was that, by this time, Schepisi had acquired a number of reliable collaborators, including his gifted cameraman Ian Baker, and music director Bruce Smeaton. Having also gained useful business skills while working in advertising, Schepisi himself would go on to arrange the distribution deals associated with the film. None of this happened fast but his background meant that he wasn't coming with virginal sensitivity to the making of his first feature. There were also some important links with *The Priest*, the segment he had directed in *Libido*, including actor Arthur Dignam, who would play another anguished priest in *Devil*, and author Thomas Keneally, screenwriter of *The Priest*, who would play a vivid role as a visiting priest in *Devil*.

SETTING THE SCENE

What would prove to be one of Schepisi's great strengths was his capacity to make the interplay of persons and environment acquire almost immediate thematic significance, as he would later reveal in a wide generic range of US films, starting with *Barbarosa* in 1982. *Devil* opens on a wide shot of verdant landscape and, in Baker's luminous cinematography, pans to where a lot of boys are playing in a river. A black-clad figure of a priest, seen from the rear, emerges to view the scene and at once the film seems to be setting up contrasting—and possibly conflicting—images: of the natural world, which encourages the boys' spontaneous frolicking, and the notion of potential restraint embodied in the figure of the priest observing it. Schepisi, speaking of this sequence, also praised the role of "Bruce Smeaton, the composer, [who] thought it was good to open with a sort of an overture as part of educating the audience as to how it's going to view the film."[27]

This may sound as if Schepisi is spelling out too explicitly what will be a key thematic element in the film, but that is not the end of this opening episode. Tom Allen (Simon Burke), who will prove to be the film's youthful protagonist, comes to ask the elderly Brother Sebastian (Charles McCallum): "Are you OK?" This benign-seeming old man is sitting on a bench in the grounds and between him and the boy we glimpse nothing but kindly concern and friendliness. Then the sequence finishes with two kids scrapping in the playground, and there's a brief whiff of the homoerotic, as one says "We can do anything we like to each other"—but not in this place, it will be quickly made clear. Even at this very early stage, there is a sense of the windows of the several-story seminary acting as a metaphor for its keeping watch on the boys' every movement. And, in the next sequence, the tormented Brother Francine (Dignam), supervising the boys' showering, reprimands Tom for washing nude, in a speech which includes the line: "The eyes are the windows of the soul and must be protected." This seems almost a verbal riff on the preceding image.

The point of giving such detail about these introductory sequences is to suggest that, from the outset, *The Devil's Playground* will have more on its mind than a simple-minded and schematic critique of an educational system that prepares boys for a religious vocation. I would suggest that it ushers in something subtler than critique: its concern is for lives being lived in certain ways that may not always be in the best interests of those living them but that cannot be simply dismissed. Though Schepisi's personal knowledge of the workings of an institution like the one depicted in the film certainly guarantees a sort of authenticity, the fact that he shook himself clear of the influence of its real-life counterpart doesn't mean that *The Devil's Playground* is an anti-Catholic diatribe. As Neil Rattigan wrote: "While Schepisi is clearly exorcising some personal devils through the seminary experiences of Tom, he is a long way removed from condemning the institution and its practices."[28] One of the most impressive qualities of the film is its even-handedness in dealing with the brotherhood. If the film comes down against the kinds of repression in the training and attitudes of the school, there is understanding and generosity as well for those lives that are bounded by it. Writing of *The Devil's Playground*, Peter Malone, a priest and film critic, felt that though admirers of Schepisi's films "might well have expected a tirade against religion or the Catholic Church or the narrowness of the Brothers' outlook . . . this does not happen."[29]

THOSE LIVES—DISCIPLINED? OR TORMENTED?

Though there is much more to the film than critical appraisal of the seminary's approach to the training of young minds or to the confinement of the brothers responsible for this, there is no denying the torment imposed on some of them by the strictures of the faith the brothers have espoused. Some of them—priests and boys—deal better with these than others.

The Brothers

Brother Francine is the most obvious embodiment of the powerful element of repression at work in the seminary. In the shower scene referred to above, he insists to the boys: "You must practice self-denial, self-discipline." It is significant that Francine (his colleagues call him "Frank," but the informality doesn't suit him) is the brother given the task of spelling out the tenets of the seminary, partly because he seems to adhere to them so rigorously and partly because, in him, the cost of the repression they enjoin is most potently rendered. For him, "the devil's playground" is essentially the body with its sexual demands, and the boys are at an age when such demands are making themselves felt acutely.

It's not just in the matter of showering that the repressive theosophy makes itself felt. The boys must undress in the morning with their bodies concealed by dressing gowns; they are constantly being raced off to Mass. (Tom is always late, because, as a bed-wetter, he has first to wash his pajamas, and what kind of repression lies behind this adolescent embarrassment?) The image of the shadowed corridors through which they run to Mass seems to stand as a visual enactment of the constraining function of the seminary, and of course, the very title, with some irony implied, hammers the nail home. "An undisciplined mind is the devil's playground," as Brother Francine intones. But it is not all made to sound as if it's being set up just to be knocked down, and there is a touching moment of thoughtfulness as Tom and his friend Turner walk through the colonnade discussing the ideals of meditation and control—in summary, the *discipline*. When Tom later rebels against—and leaves—the life of the seminary, one remembers such earlier occasions when he at least gave the demands of the discipline mind-room. As Rattigan insightfully wrote: "The theme of growing up is nearly always associated with the theme of innocence, and the journey to maturity nearly always invokes some sense of its loss," but goes on to say: "What Tom sheds is ignorance or the artificial fostering of innocence that the seminary encourages."[30]

When we turn to the brothers themselves, those who have accepted the rigorous demands of their lives, at least in lip service to their vows and in the largely secluded life they have opted for, we find that the notion of repression and its challenges is far from uniformly articulated. At a moment towards the end of the film, following the discovery of the drowned body of a spiritually tormented boy, Brother Francine says: "There's nothing wrong with us, is there?" By this stage of the film, we might be tempted to add: "And look who's talking!"

The brothers are well-differentiated, physically and in terms of character and how they handle the discipline of their vocations, reminding one of that belief of Schepisi's quoted above about "the full range of personalities" likely to be found in any institution. First billed in the credits is Arthur Dignam, and it is appropriate that he should be so, because he is the one who epitomizes most vividly the conflict the vocation can set up. Physically, Dignam is lean almost to the point of emaciation, even if, in a later anguished moment, he says: "I've got a damned good body . . . but no one's seen it in years, let alone touch it." The point of his physical appearance is to stress the kind of discipline to which he has subjected himself. Whereas the other brothers may be seen to relax, to smile, Francine presents always a dour personal image. He not only articulates the necessary rigors of the order but seems at first the one whose life most nearly conforms to these. In the common room episodes when the brothers gather communally, he is apt to be at a remove from the more convivial chat of the others. In virtually all Schepisi's later films, placement of several characters in a key setting proves a potent mode of differentiation.

However, we haven't seen all of Francine yet; that is, we've glimpsed only the surface of repression—the physically austere figure given to strict utterance. On a day when the boys are going off on an excursion and some of the brothers are having a leisure break and letting off steam in various ways, Francine goes to a swimming pool in a neighboring town. He has been planning, he maintains, a nice quiet day. At the pool, in the changing room as well as poolside, his conflicts between the body's sensuality (both male and female bodies come in for the camera's scrutiny) and the suppressions of religion are forcibly enacted. The others in the men's dressing room strip and change unselfconsciously, as Francine discreetly inserts his spartan frame into his swimming trunks. Once outside, he eyes the women in their bathing costumes, with cleavage to the fore, and can't keep his eye off the legs exposed under the doors of the women's changing room. He then sits in cramped anguish on a lavatory seat, presumably lost in contemplation of his riven nature.

Near the end of the film, he announces in the priests' study/sitting room: "I hate life. It's evil. . . . The body dominates the mind." This pronouncement is reflected in his dreams, in which he imagines himself nude, joining underwater a group of young women swimming similarly unattired. When an interviewer described Francine as "a very

extreme characterization," Schepisi replied, "That's what you think....
I can tell you that the Arthur Dignam character is a mere shadow of
a couple of the people I experienced," further claiming that he had
responses from many who'd attended a Catholic boarding school
and would insist: "There was one in every school, and they would
say to me, 'Oh, you were kind to him.'"[31] It is, in fact, one of the film's
strengths that it allows for a range of priestly behavior and responses,
and even the representation of Francine is not entirely without some
sense of sympathy for the way the man's life has been so conflicted.

The first of the priests we meet is the elderly and genial old Brother
Sebastian, whom Tom greets in the early episode discussed above, and
in other sequences, some of them set in the brothers' common room,
Schepisi has allowed for a range of types. They are seen enjoying each
other's company—and a glass of whiskey or a cigarette or both—or
playing billiards or singing (not hymns, either!) We are not here in the
sentimental territory of, say, *Going My Way*, but in a humanely rendered
realization that there is more to these men than their vows. For instance,
while Francine is at the pool, the more genial Brother Victor (Nick Tate)
and the studious junior, Brother James (Peter Cox), have first enjoyed
themselves at a football match where they blend in with the rest of
the crowd, dressed as they are in mufti and therefore not recognizably
"different." Barracking for their team scarcely constitutes a sin against
the order of the brotherhood, but when they repair to a crowded pub
after the match, a somewhat riskier letting-off of steam takes place, for
Vic especially. There are two women sitting nearby (Anne Phelan, Jillian
Archer), and Vic, by this time well-oiled and attracted by cleavage and
other hints of ready femininity, leads James to join them. One of the
girls claims she'd like "a bit of fun," and, as Vic and Jim get back to their
car, Vic, who's had his hands on the woman's shoulder, says: "They nearly
had me." What this little episode dramatizes is the sheer precariousness
of the repression the brothers are forced to practice, and the added fact
that Vic crashes the car on the way back to the seminary reinforces the
point. When the constraints of the seminary are off, the results are apt
to be excessive and possibly dangerous for them.

The other brothers all get an individuating moment or two,
sometimes in the classroom or conducting the choir, or when the
elderly Brother Sebastian sits in the common room companionably

drinking tea with the other elderly brother, Hanrahan (Gerry Duggan), while Victor is getting into the whiskey. Small touches like these help to distinguish the black-clad brothers: beneath the uniform of the order, and whatever its disciplines, they retain some *essence* of self, and this sense of character is one of the film's strengths. Without their being drawn as fully rounded characters, they are physically as well as psychologically distinguished from each other. In Schepisi's words, "I had a belief that it's good to cast sculpturally, so that you're physically casting different shapes and sizes."[32] The result is that the brothers are well-differentiated, both physically and in terms of character and how they handle the discipline of their vocations.

The visiting Father Marshall (Thomas Keneally), who has come to the seminary to conduct a retreat, seems by contrast with the resident brothers to be acting a part—or, rather, at least a couple of parts. Tediously jovial in the common room, he also acts the role of sympathetic counselor to the boys, trying to draw them out on "any problems you can't talk about," or to get Tom to talk about "temptations you find hard to handle." Then, when the retreat gets underway, the beaming confidant role gives way to the scarifying zealot and saver of souls: "the body we pamper will become a city of corruption. . . . If we lose our battle with temptation we shall be lost forever more." His sermon is, as Pauline Kael described it, "pure fundamentalist hellfire and damnation, holding up to the boys the images such as a fiery worm consuming their entrails for eternity, and real terror hovers in the air."[33] This recalls the terrifying images of hell James Joyce's retreat-preacher put before the students in *A Portrait of the Artist as a Young Man*. By chance, the UK/Irish film version of Joyce's great novel was released within a few months of *The Devil's Playground*.[34] In it, the retreat sermons were given a tour de force rendering by John Gielgud, but, as he is not seen in the wider community of the seminary as Keneally's Father Marshall is, there is not the same opportunity for comparing his on- and off-stage personae. Marshall's incessant geniality when he's not performing arguably allows us a more comprehensive account of the visiting priest. Keneally described it as "a common double role we'd encountered in our childhoods, Fred's and mine."[35] He wrote the sermon, but otherwise Schepisi wrote the screenplay, though with some "uncredited assistance" from Keneally.

Kael's summarizing comments about how the brothers are represented seem wholly apt: "The film gives you the impression that Schepisi has got the whole thing right. He must have freed himself very thoroughly: this isn't an anti-Catholic movie. Far from it. Schepisi loves these tormented comedians [i.e., the brothers]. But he looks at them with humorous pagan eyes."[36]

The Boys

Inevitably perhaps, the brothers are more clearly differentiated from each other than is the case with the boys, for whom "The training school is both a challenge and a constraint . . . a home and a prison."[37] These boys, all dealing with adolescence as well as with the demands of their professed vocation, are at more or less the same stage of their development. Even so, several of them, as well as Tom, stand out from their grey-uniformed contemporaries to make their presences felt in ways that matter to the film's agenda. For example, the older boy Fitz (John Diedrich), a friend of Tom's, seems cheerfully well-adjusted, and his usual easiness with the brotherhood helps to highlight by contrast Tom's growing tensions. When he too finally leaves the seminary, this makes Tom's departure less wholly a matter of a single rebellion than a considered critique of a system that "show[s] the counter-productivity of rigid rules."[38]

If the seemingly easygoing Fitz finds the rules more than he can conform to, perhaps they do indeed need loosening. The other boy who emerges with tragic clarity is Turner. A friend of Tom's has warned him against Turner ("He's nuts"), and the introverted, tormented Turner will eventually be found when the lake is dragged. His fate is the most damning commentary that Schepisi makes, and as one review had it: "the film, for all its lyricism and understanding, carries a sharp edge of criticism."[39]

Tom may finally turn his back on the seminary (as Schepisi himself did), but the film's intelligence doesn't run to black-and-white distinctions. It offers a reflection rather than a polemic in its dealings with both priests and boys. There is critique, yes, in which the life of the seminary makes problematic demands on both, but it never descends to being an anti-Catholic rant.

The "Devil" at Large

In hindsight, of course, *Devil* is the film that really launched Schepisi as an Australian—and later international—filmmaker, but despite receiving some critical plaudits, it was not a box-office success at the time of its release. It had difficulty in finding a place in the Australian cinema chains of the time, in spite of having been a success at the 1976 Cannes Film Festival: it was the only Australian film selected for "Directors' Fortnight," and it was lauded as "one of the four finest films in the Directors' Section" by London's *Daily Telegraph*.[40] The film had to wait five years for release in the US. However, Pauline Kael was impressed by the way, early in the film, "the full wide-screen images glide by" in articulation of Schepisi's "own softly rhythmed style," summing up the movie as "this great Australian film."[41] Since its disappointing release, subsequent accounts of the film tend to bolster its initially high reputation. In novelist Christos Tsiolkas's book-length study of the film, he recalled how the film had enthralled him first as a boy of thirteen at the time of its release. Then again in 1989, he found that though it "explores a very small moment in time . . . it does so with a grace and refreshing truthfulness that, I think, will make Tom Allen a permanent figure in our collective landscape."[42] Later still, in 2000, at the time of writing, he sums up its effect as follows: "The film itself plays out as a series of movements, each one increasingly drawing Tom into a circle from which he will force himself to flee. This fleeing is Tom's liberation because it indicates that his conscious will has finally caught up to the rebelliousness and spirit of his body."[43] As a summary of the film's narrative route, that is probably as eloquent and incisive as we could expect. It is not essentially a critical study of the film, but it is an engaging account of how a particular film may enrich a person's life experience—and at various stages of that life—while evoking much of the film's visual and aural impact. Tsiolkas distinguishes acutely among the differing tensions and temptations that emerge among both the boys and the brothers, and, in repudiating the auteur theory, claims "that the editor, the performer, the cinematographer and the scriptwriter have as much to do with the pleasures of movie going as does the director."[44] To which list, in relation to *The Devil's Playground*, he would also pay special tribute to the contribution of Bruce Smeaton's score. Tsiolkas's is a very personal, sometimes idiosyncratic approach to Schepisi's film, but it remains one of the most insightful on several levels, thematic and creative.

The Devil's Playground established Schepisi, along with others such as Peter Weir, Bruce Beresford, and Gillian Armstrong, as a key figure in the Australian film revival. And, like those other directors, he would go on to enjoy a productive decade or so of filmmaking in the US and the UK. In recent years, there has been a good deal of publicity relating to abuse in Catholic institutions, especially in boarding schools. Schepisi's film acknowledges the constraints of life in Tom's seminary, but never falls into the trap of implying that there was nothing else to be said for it.

Chapter Three

A "MASTER-WORK"—THE CHANT OF JIMMIE BLACKSMITH

FRED SCHEPISI AND TOM KENEALLY

In the lead-up to this movie so eulogistically described by US critic Pauline Kael as "the great Australian film *The Chant of Jimmie Blacksmith*,"[1] Schepisi had acquired a huge boost in critical status. This derived from the Australian Film Institute's conferring of six awards for *The Devil's Playground* (1976), and he also came garlanded with praise from the film's screening at Cannes. As noted in the previous chapter, Schepisi had first made contact with author Thomas Keneally when working on the 1963 portmanteau film, *Libido*. Keneally was one of those writers in other media that the company behind *Libido* wanted to lure into screenwriting. Keneally had written the screenplay for Schepisi's segment, *The Priest*, and in *The Devil's Playground* he played the visiting priest, Father Marshall. Furthermore, according to one reputable source, he gave uncredited assistance on the screenplay.[2] Having shared a truncated seminary background with Schepisi, he had gone on to become an award-winning novelist, and in 1972 he was short-listed for the Man Booker Prize for *The Chant of Jimmie Blacksmith*. Schepisi recalled being so impressed by Keneally's story for *Libido* that, as he said, "I grabbed it straight off the bat, I wanted to meet him because I knew he was writing *The Chant of Jimmie Blacksmith*."[3]

Keneally's novel, which Schepisi himself adapted, seeking advice from Keneally, was based on factual events relating to an Aboriginal called Jimmy Governor, and both novel and film "examined black/white relationships in Australia's early colonial days when the detribalized black was an easy mark for the white supremacist boot."[4] The latter 1970s saw a rash of adaptations of Australian novels, both classic and popular, and these were indeed very influential in the revival of Australian cinema in that decade. Titles such as *Picnic at Hanging Rock* (Peter Weir, 1975), *The Getting of Wisdom* (Bruce Beresford, 1977) and *My Brilliant Career* (Gillian Armstrong, 1979) often highlighted the idea of young people coming to terms with their environments and their futures. *The Chant of Jimmie Blacksmith* both does and does not fit easily into this context. Schepisi's film had a harsh realism in its depiction of Jimmie's coming of age, and the film's tone was in keeping with the brutal reality of an Aboriginal youth seeking a place in an alien community. According to Neil Rattigan, "the film broke the bonds of genteel period reconstruction that had characterized the New Australian Cinema to that time."[5] This chapter will examine its place in the revival as well as its intrinsic qualities and what they reveal of Schepisi's development before the next major phase of his career.

When one considers that the actual events, as in the film, took place in 1900, it is tempting to identify another element of the coming-of-age theme in the fact that, in this same year, Australian states embraced Federation, surely a crucial step in its move towards some kind of nationhood. The six Australian states, hitherto British "colonies," were given royal assent to the Commonwealth of Australia Constitution Act in July 1900, and it was proclaimed on January 1, 1901. There had been some opposition to the idea of Federation, but none of it was likely to have been based on the rights of Aboriginal ownership of the land, which white settlement in general had little notion of. In Schepisi's film, it is worth considering the tone of references to Federation and how these tie in with the individual drama of Jimmie Blacksmith's conflicted life and "declaration of war" on the white world that instructs him but denies him a place. There is some suggestion of parallel between white Australia's shaking off its colonial past and Jimmie's own rites of passage as he tries to adjust himself to a different world. "Coming of age" doesn't necessarily involve the erasure of times past, nor does it make good the promise of things to come.

JIMMY GOVERNOR

The tragic real-life history of Aboriginal Jimmy Governor involves "events leading to the massacre and violent rampage in which altogether twelve white people were murdered, raped and seriously injured," writes historian Henry Reynolds.[6] Jimmy Governor, of mixed descent, was born in 1875 and was hanged for murder in New South Wales in 1901, following outbursts of homicidal violence the year before. Keneally's novel and subsequently Schepisi's film, while not purporting to be works of history, draw heavily on the key events in Governor's life. Like Jimmie Blacksmith, Governor had had some "white" education, was literate, and worked in the white world as a fence-builder among other occupations, including a brief stint as a police trooper.

He seems to have been aware of his difference from many Black men of his day and of his age, certainly at least in the perception of the white employers for whom he worked, and to have encouraged this sense of difference. In this matter, the actor Tommy Lewis, who starred as Schepisi's Jimmie, echoed Governor in a 2008 interview when he claimed that playing Blacksmith saved him from the fate of his contemporaries, so many of whom were then dead or turned to alcoholism. "I am not a Black fella and I'm not a white fella. So, who am I? Where do I belong?" he said, recalling both of his forebears: the real-life Jimmy and the novel's (and film's) Jimmie.[7] Like the latter, Governor also impregnated and married a white girl, Ethel, and this was not considered an outrage; the exercise of male lust on women, white or Black, was simply accepted. The elements of racism and sexism involved in such views would not have made impact in those distant days.

The "Mawbey murders" were no doubt the turning point in Jimmy Governor's life, just as the "Newby" crimes are in Keneally's and Schepisi's dramatizations. He worked at fencing on Mawbey's property and was generally well regarded by his employer, but dealing with the Mawbey women, who derided Ethel for her marriage to an Aboriginal, was a fraught business that led to their murder. Historian Reynolds, on the basis of Jimmy's testimony during his trial, believes that the evidence suggests that Jimmy "had planned no outrage. His intention was only to confront Mrs. Mawbey, in the absence of her husband, and to warn her to stop insulting Ethel."[8]

Reynolds's book, while sometimes alert to such filmic achievements as the visual impact of the opening scenes, represents essentially a historian's approach to both Keneally's novel and Schepisi's film. When pondering his response to the film, he asks: "Should it be considered as history or as fiction?"[9] On the whole, viewing the film from the perspective of his own discipline, he is apt to take issue with its dealing with the facts of the life from which both novel and film were derived, claiming that they "inform us more about the 1970s than the late nineteenth century. We learn more of the film-maker and the writer than we do about Jimmy Governor and his brother."[10] Well, films always tell us (not necessarily in didactic mode) about the times in which they are made, in matters large and small, and *The Chant of Jimmie Blacksmith* is no exception.

It is not my aim to give a detailed account of Jimmy Governor's short tragic life, but just to make clear that the narrative trajectory of Schepisi's film, though formally adapted from Keneally's novel, also draws its impetus from historical facts. The film's range of characters, as well as its key events, have their origin not just in Keneally's celebrated novel but the actual material of Jimmy Governor's life, though it does not have to—and does not—adhere to them in ways that a historian might require. Regardless of its real-life affiliations, *The Chant of Jimmie Blacksmith* is a narrative and a drama, not a tract.

FROM PAGE TO SCREEN

In relation to those key film adaptations that helped establish the Australian film revival of the 1970s, I many years ago wrote of Schepisi's version of Keneally's novel: "Each provides an impressive telling of a serious, in fact important, story. Each shares a committed, passionate view of the hopelessly inhumane suppression of one race by another as it develops its narrative of Aboriginal Jimmie Blacksmith's aspirations to white culture and the subverting of these [that] leads to his taking a terrible revenge."[11]

KENEALLY'S NOVEL

Jimmie is, as Jimmy Governor was, only half-Aboriginal: he had a white father who, as seems to have been common, had his way with a Black woman. However, the statement does sum up the film's narrative structure, derived as it is from Keneally's novel (and the story of the real-life Jimmy), in that the first half chronicles Jimmie's attempts to find his way in the white world, and the second to the aftermath of his massacre of the women of the white family that has employed him. What Keneally has achieved in spare, evocative prose, Schepisi and his cinematographer, Ian Baker, will render in audio-visual images of compelling power.

The novel starts by recording that, in June 1900, Jimmie's uncle "was disturbed to get news that Jimmie had married a white girl in the Methodist church of Wallah,"[12] and he sets out to take to Jimmie the tooth that had been knocked out as part of his tribal initiation rites in 1891. A good deal of the novel's central conflict is foreshadowed in these opening pages: that is, Jimmie as a half-caste may aspire to the white culture that has brought much suffering to the indigenous population, but he will not find it easy to shake off the Aboriginal world in which he has grown up.

In chapter two, a well-meaning Methodist clergyman, the Reverend Neville—the mission station superintendent who, with his wife, has taken Jimmie under his wing—tries to encourage Jimmie by saying: "If you could ever find a nice girl off a farm to marry, your children would only be quarter-caste then, and your grandchildren one-eighth caste, scarcely black at all" (p. 7). And this is about as sympathetic an approach to Jimmie's situation as he will receive. After working for several white bosses, Jimmie feels that "he had a license to run mad" (p. 76), and he embarks on a massacre of the family of one of those bosses, Mr. Newby. From then on, he, along with full-blood Aboriginal brother Mort, is on the run, "becoming a figure of myth" (p. 137). While he is in flight, the wider historical context involves talk of the Boer War, in which other racial conflict is leading to terrible loss of life, and of the Federation project that will proclaim Australia an independent country (rather than a collection of six colonies), a movement that will do nothing for the Aboriginal population that the whites have consigned to the remote outskirts of the land. Keneally recently gave his view as to the relevance of Federation to his novel in these terms: "The fact that Federation was happening at the time of the Boer War was significant because that war was Britain's disgrace, especially to someone of Irish grand-parentage [as he was]. It was England's Vietnam in that the rest of the world was appalled by it."[13]

THE FILM

Getting Started

The film, as suggested above, adheres quite closely to the novel's structural procedures, but its coherence derives equally from its visual qualities, which so potently render its tragic conflicts and their outcome. Schepisi has chosen to open with a fuzzy shot of an Aboriginal camp that proves to be the view of the Reverend Neville (Jack Thompson) from inside his house, observing the Black camp through thin curtains. This is followed by long shots of landscape, ominous close-ups of rocks and jagged trees, and of an Aboriginal initiation ritual. At once—and this is all part of a pre-credit sequence—a contrast of two kinds of life, Black and white, interior and exterior, is announced. The young Jimmie, object of the ritual, is recalled by Neville and, because of his having absented himself from the "higher things," Neville beats him. Jimmie is at this stage just a little boy, and in hindsight this beating from an often-sympathetic white man may seem to resonate as the precursor of the later violence Jimmie will wreak on his white employers. It also introduces Schepisi's ongoing preoccupation with the lot of outsiders: Jimmie, half-caste, cannot easily accommodate to either of the lifestyles the film has already adumbrated, neither the uninhibited world of the Black camp with its rituals and noisy activity, nor the "civilized" interior of the Nevilles' home, with its books, curtains, and cushioned chairs.

Jimmie as Outsider

Immediately after the credits and the title that reads, "Based on real events that took place at the turn of the century," the older Jimmie (Tommy Lewis) is depicted as being at odds with the Aboriginal culture in which he has grown up. White boys give/sell liquor to the Blacks, and one of them presses Jimmie to drink "to make a man of you." Jimmie spits it out, and when armed police ride by he hides, his observing face given in apprehensive close-up. An older Black man also urges Jimmie to drink, claiming, "You've been with that reverend too long." With shrewd visual and aural economy, Schepisi has established the conflicting claims on his growing-up. Minutes later, he is seen at the meal table in the Reverend Neville's house where the minister urges Jimmie to stay away from those drinks and to think of marrying a white girl. These words of advice elicit thanks from Jimmie: "You and Mrs. Neville have give me good education." The camera then pulls away from the table to observe Jimmie flanked by the pastor and his dour wife (Julie Dawson), while most of the screen is filled with a dull confining green wall. The resulting image suggests that white approval has been bought at the cost of this oppressiveness. And as Neil Rattigan wrote, Jimmie is "a central character ... caught between two mutually uncomprehending cultures."[14]

In his efforts to find a place in the white man's world, Jimmie takes on a series of jobs, including working on an orchard for Healey (Tim Robertson), who threatens him, if he should prove unsatisfactory, by saying, "I'll cut your bloody black balls off." Sparing in his praise, when Jimmie is later digging and installing slab fences, he allows grudgingly: "Not too bad at all." Otherwise, Healy and his wife (Jane Harders) barely acknowledge his presence and, soon after, Healy unfairly dismisses him and strikes him. But back in the Aboriginal camp, Jimmie looks morosely at odds with the others as they go drinking and shouting. In this way, the film punctuates his attempts to find acceptance in the white world with returns to the Black one, where he no longer feels at home, and, at one point, Baker's camera catches in close-up a look in his eye that seems to say: "I'm about to leave."

His next job finds him working as a tracker with a police officer, Farrell (Ray Barrett), who is an alcoholic and has sexually dubious habits. Jimmie tries to draw him out on the subject of Federation, venturing, "Good thing, boss," and getting in reply: "Yeah, but not for you Black bastards. Wouldn't be any different for you Black bastards.... I suppose you'd still have the same rights. None!" Farrell laughing loudly at his own "wit." Writing about the issue of Federation, a UK reviewer noted that "the point Schepisi repeatedly underlines is that the uncertainty of the state's white colonial society, both about its own identity and the concept of 'nationhood,' was counterbalanced by a conviction that the Aboriginal had no real place either in his ancestral homeland or in the soon-to-be-born Commonwealth of

Australia."[15] Farrell's crude words on the subject may seem to reinforce Jimmie's outsider status, but they also echo the white preoccupation with its own status. While working with Farrell, they ride into a Black settlement, and Jimmie finds himself at odds with his own people, striking out at them and bringing one into the jail, where he will be hanged. Jimmie, by now, is both drawn to and corrupted by white ways and is no longer at one with Black habits. A poignant moment occurs when the Black man, Harry Edwards, imprisoned by Farrell, hangs himself. Jimmie cuts the man down, lays him on a bench and tenderly covers his dead body. No longer able to cope with his conflicted situation, he burns his uniform. He may hanker for some aspects of white men's ways, but the cruel death of a Black man, for whose capture he has been partly responsible, is something he finds too hard to bear.

The turning point in his quest for employment with whites comes when he is taken on by the seemingly decent Jack Newby (Don Crosby), for whom he works at fence-building and as assistant in the shearing shed. In the latter, there is casual racist talk ("I thought you darkies went barefoot, Jacko," one shearer offers patronizingly to Jimmie) and talk about how Britain "declared war" in South Africa, a phrase that Jimmie will later use when he embarks on his revenge agenda. Newby's household includes two sons and a wife (Ruth Cracknell), daughters, and a woman schoolteacher Petra Graf (Elizabeth Alexander), who lives with them.

Meanwhile Jimmie has made love to a rather dim white girl, Gilda (Angela Punch), whom he marries when she becomes pregnant. The Newbys have been reasonably kind to Gilda, who gives birth in their homestead. "You can have your little one at my place," Mrs. Newby tells her, advising Gilda to come to her if Jimmie ever beats her, a possibility Gilda rebuts. The situation changes radically when the baby proves not to be his. The child is obviously white: "I really thought he was yours," she tearfully asserts, and Jimmie, now feeling out of both Black and white worlds, fears: "He won't want to know me when he grows up." The Newbys' instinctive racism is fanned by the return of Jimmie's brother Mort (Freddy Reynolds), with two other Aboriginals, leading Mr. Newby finally to yell: "You and your tribe can pack up and get."

Declaring War

Structure may seem somewhat loose as Jimmie moves from one situation to another, but it can also be argued that the film's narrative procedure to this turning point at the Newbys' farm enacts his attempts to find his way in a white world that is far from being universally welcoming. As one critic wrote, though the film "proceeds in a leisurely manner," this is offset by "an undercurrent of fear [that] runs powerfully through the whole film"[16] and helps to account for its coherence. Almost exactly halfway through the film, Jimmie has been pushed beyond his endurance by the treatment he has received. Miss Graf has warned Gilda: "You'll only lose that child if you stay with the Blacks." When Mrs. Newby turns Jimmie away, he confronts Newby who refuses to pay him or give him food. He then goes on a rampage, knocking Mrs. Newby down, hacking at Petra and the other white girls. Echoing the earlier statement about how war was declared in South Africa, he announces, after his massacre of the Newby women, "I've declared war."

This episode is brilliantly filmed by Schepisi and his collaborators, notably cinematographer Baker and editor Brian Kavanagh. We are here a long way from the CGI-dominated violence of so much modern popular cinema. Kavanagh recalled that "a single take didn't work; there was no tension in it, so the editing was done as a combination of long takes and hand-held material."[17] Each shot is managed so as to make its point and its contribution to the overall sense of the terrible carnage that Jimmie's outrage has led to. It is achieved in a rapid montage of close-up details interspersed with whole-screen shots to render the summation of those close-ups, as, for instance, the camera cuts from Tommy Lewis's face to an axe landing on a woman's shoulder. It is horrifying and had to be, but as Schepisi has said: "I wanted it to be an anti-violence moment" and "not a balletic blood-letting."[18] In other words, we register the violence as horrifying and are given the evidence we need for this, but, as well, the film forces us to be repelled by it, and in this sense it serves Schepisi's "anti-violence" motive.

What is also remarkable is the way in which, without in any sense absolving Jimmie of responsibility for this outbreak, it never lets us forget the series of events, the racist slurs and patronage, the sense of outsider status that haunts him, that have led him to it. He urges Gilda to pack, hurry and leave, and moves his Black relations—Mort, Uncle Tabidgi, and cousin Peter—away. As they journey through a rugged landscape with daunting rock faces, he makes his declaration of "war," and for the rest of the film he will be in pursuit by white posses, sometimes with the harsh irony of an Aboriginal member among these pursuers.

On the Run

As with the first half of the film, what follows the turning point of the massacre is more than what might seem superficially to be a somewhat straggling series of events. However, as with those earlier scenes, it is essentially given coherence by the interest Schepisi maintains in how Jimmie responds to the ongoing challenges of his life. And these include his dealings with his giggling brother Mort, the sense of dangerous release his rampage at the Newby home has bequeathed him, and an intricate relationship with schoolteacher McCready, whom he takes as "hostage," though that term doesn't do justice to the subtleties that underpin his connection to Jimmie's emerging self. Jimmie's is the wildest of the coming-of-age or rite-of-passage narratives that were so prevalent in the new Australian cinema of the 1970s, but his has been the most taxing that any protagonist has had to deal with. He has left an environment in which he could not feel "at home" and has, with tragic and horrific results, failed in his quest for another way.

In the latter half of the film, "Jimmie Blacksmith" has become a household name. In a butcher's shop a self-important customer (Arthur Dignam, in his third performance in a Schepisi film) asserts: "Jimmie Blacksmith—his name's known throughout the state. The whole country's looking for him." It's as though this provides excitement for the likes of this customer who goes on to say to the butcher (Brian Anderson), who is also the hangman: "You've got a ringside seat to history." In a nicely subtle touch, the butcher is a decent-seeming, reserved man who claims: "I'm just part of the apparatus." The court case, at which Gilda is present in the company of nuns, produces a guilty verdict against the still-fleeing Jimmie and obviously brings further public attention to the runaways, and, when they fetch up at the home of the teacher, McCready (Peter Carroll) and his wife (Robyn Nevin), a copy of the *Bulletin* magazine announces: "Blacksmith brothers still at large after two months."

Interspersed among such moments that establish the growing renown of the fugitives is the spectacle of their running through rigorous landscapes of dead trees or threatening rock formations. Accompanied now only by Mort, Jimmie embarks on subsequent rampages. As they approach one isolated house, they walk on the fence rails so as not to leave footprints, in one of those details Schepisi so perceptively includes to lend credence to the events. By now, Mort, who is not in the same racially conflicted state as his half-brother but has become wilder from the experience, constantly yelling or cackling with laughter, weeps at their plight after the shooting of a woman. When Jimmie says, "They expect me to do wrong... they're disappointed if we don't," Mort turns against him.

While the film deals tellingly in both narrative and visual terms with the flight, in Schepisi's direction, and under the terms of his screenplay, there is also an underlying poignancy in the realization that there is a growing sense of how it has been internalized in the natures of—and relationship between—the two brothers. And these matters will move towards an unravelling when the brothers fetch up at McCready's house. "You don't have to think you have to kill us," the teacher quietly tries to reason with them, and his face in close-up renders the fear that comes with the prospect of being taken as their hostage.

McCready, as skillfully played by Peter Carroll, is perhaps the most interesting character in the film. He seems a little prissy talking about how sweating leads to catching cold, but he also shows a kind of reasonableness in his attempts to dissuade Jimmie from further violence—and a firmer grasp of the racial conflict in Australia. "I can understand your being angry," he says, and the conversation turns, perhaps more explicitly than is needed, to the foregrounding of the film's political stance. Whereas Aborigines were said to have killed four or five thousand whites, McCready tells Jimmie: "You might ask how many Aborigines did the whites kill—270,000."

Now, it may appear that the teacher is being used as the film's liberal mouthpiece, but in Carroll's subtle playing this emerges as part of his intellectual appraisal of a vile political situation, and its effect on Jimmie's thinking is crucial to the film's determination not to oversimplify such issues. Jimmie claims that the whites "took away a way of life. What have we done?" and McCready's satirical reply is: "You can't say we haven't given you anything. We introduced you to alcohol, religion, influenza, measles, syphilis, schools—a whole host of improvements." If there is a didactic potential here, it is offset by Carroll's imbuing it with a touch of sardonic character and a concern for leading Jimmie to a fuller understanding of the larger world, of which the landscape becomes a threatening metaphor. "No one does a murder because he wants to."

Increasingly the landscape looks more awesome. When the little party of Jimmie, Mort, and McCready arrives at an Aboriginal ground, they are met with huge and menacing rocks, superbly shot, that look both monstrous and precarious. The site has been defaced by white crudities, one of which proclaims: "Fuck Federation," and from this place Jimmie flees, following McCready's urging that Mort is not really his brother, and Mort looks after the ailing teacher, delivering him to his home, before running off to fall victim to survivors of the Newby massacre. The intricacy of racial hatred and the burgeoning nation that has been built on this is apt to recall John Ford's magisterial Western *The Searchers*, with which Schepisi's film also shares a profound grasp of the mixed beauty and terror of the landscape.

The End = What?

As the avenging horsemen draw near Jimmie, he jumps in a river, is shot in the face but not killed, applies a mud poultice to the wound, and continues his flight. But he is now nearing his physical extreme and, when he is dragged away by the seekers from the convent where he has made his unnoticed way in, he has come to an end that can only leave us wondering what it has meant in personal and wider terms. He will be hanged, but has his "declaration of war" made any impact on the white community, other than that of horror? Has that community learned anything about its situation in the near-Federation country that has such a history of brutal oppression of the long-term owners of the country?

Taking us back to the film's start, the Reverend Neville reappears, and visiting Jimmie in jail he claims to feel "very responsible" for what has happened: "We don't feel it's entirely your fault." So, the film leaves us pondering the element of white guilt for Jimmie's dreadful maraudings. The final image is one of a vast and challenging landscape from which birds fly upwards. This seems to me an image of deliberate ambiguity: it is devoid of all signs of the human habitation that has produced such moral chaos, but does the birds' flight also suggest that there may be further possibilities?

...

Schepisi had difficulty in funding *Jimmie Blacksmith*, and when its eventual budget "turned out to be A$1.2 million, the biggest ever for an Australian film at the time, the industry was watching, along with a media eager for controversy."[19] Despite being well received critically, the film did not fare well at the box office. Perhaps this was not the sort of image of Australia that filmgoers wanted to see in the later 1970s. It was visually and thematically more challenging than those other films that helped to launch the Australian film revival, and issues of racism had still some way to go before the gestures towards reconciliation with, and respect for, the Aboriginal community would be made in the ensuing decades.

Schepisi's clear-minded apprehension and rendering of a terrible situation now suggests that he was ahead of his time. As Keneally recalled: "Fred was considered very daring then for trying to raise a huge amount of money for a film about Aboriginals. There was always a sort of unease about its edginess and violence, about the project itself. It was a film that rubbed your face in the national disgrace. It didn't do well at the box office because that wasn't the sort of novelty people wanted; they wanted films that gave us a burnished identity in some way. I could tell it was going to shock people."[20] Henry Reynolds, despite his demurs about the film's variable relation to historical fact and to how "Schepisi allows the narrative drive of [the latter half] of the film to be diverted,"[21] allowed that "Schepisi's powerful film was undoubtedly confronting and deeply disturbing to many people,"[22] and it is likely that these are not responses that make for box-office success. Forty years later, the film seems prescient in its critique of prejudice and in the subsequent legislation that would seek to deal with this. That is the kind of idea I had in mind when earlier claiming that films inevitably reflect the times of their production; Keneally's film offers insight into racial history in Australia in the late nineteenth century and how it may have been considered in the 1970s.

Interviewed some years later and asked what had attracted him to Keneally's book in the first place, Schepisi answered: "The story of a man at odds with the system who just wants to be himself and get on with the system."[23] It will be worth keeping this reply in mind as we turn to some of his other films made in other countries.

Chapter Four

MAKING IT OVERSEAS

Like several of those directors responsible for the Australian film revival of the 1970s—including Peter Weir, Bruce Beresford, Philip Noyce, and Gillian Armstrong—Schepisi made his way to the US and the UK during the 1980s. Again mirroring those colleagues, he adapted to different working conditions, took on genres associated with their overseas situations, scored some memorable successes, and returned intermittently to film in his home territory.

Schepisi's background in commercials and documentaries made for his own company, Film House, in Australia had given him an insight into the business side of filmmaking and his two Australian features, *The Devil's Playground* and *The Chant of Jimmie Blacksmith*, had involved him in the difficulties of fundraising to get films off the ground. As he said of his venturing overseas: "I thought if I went to the US I might get films funded and win a sort of notoriety, so that when I came back here [Australia] it might make it easier for me to get money. And I also thought there might be something I could learn that I didn't know."[1] In any event, he didn't come back until 1988, and until now has made only two further films in Australia. While working in the US, he adjusted to the ways in which the industry functioned, saying: "You have to have irons in several fires over there. In Australia, you say, 'I want to make that film,' and then all the energies go into raising the money and producing that film. In America you need a number of projects . . . and you need to have very good agents and lawyers."[2] The first of those "irons" that got past the "project" stage was *Barbarosa*, and he could scarcely have embraced a more American genre to start his trans-Pacific career. No doubt the presence of two of his most distinguished collaborators, cinematographer Ian Baker and music director Bruce Smeaton, contributed a sense of community in this different filmmaking territory.

BARBAROSA (1982)

A Western?

On the surface, it may have seemed daring for an Australian director to tackle a Western for his US debut, especially at a time when the genre was somewhat in decline, and he would run into some production difficulties along the way. The catastrophic box-office (and, largely, critical) failure of Michael Cimino's *Heaven's Gate* (1980) had clearly not helped the genre's status in the early '80s. It was no longer a dominant genre as it had been in the days of, say, John Ford and Howard Hawks. Vincent Canby's review of *Barbarosa* carried the heading: "Can an Australian Revive the Western?"[3] but Janet Maslin considered that Schepisi's "foreignness in this instance [i.e., dealing with 'an American legend'] works to his great advantage."[4]

There was a good deal of reported difficulty in setting up production, despite "its $10 million dollar budget—far in excess of any Australian-produced film [at the time]"[5] and in arranging release. One of its chief distributors, Universal, described it as "a complete disaster" and refused to spend any more money on its release.[6] Schepisi's task was "to get the film to New York where his name [was] known and the depth of the film [was] more likely to be appreciated."[7]

So, whatever its inherent qualities, *Barbarosa* was not going to enjoy an easy run with the viewing public. In terms of the Western's ailing popularity, perhaps, as one writer noted: "Since Vietnam, the perception of the frontier ethic had changed. The pioneer has become imperialist and anti-ecology. The cowboy has become the Ugly American."[8] However, *Barbarosa*, among its mixed notices, at least won accolades from such prominent critics as Pauline Kael and Canby, and, nearly forty years later, it holds up well as an eloquent venture in the genre—and as a notable title in Schepisi's filmography.

As to thematic continuities, it can be said that *Barbarosa* echoes some of the preoccupations that made *Jimmie Blacksmith* such a powerful piece of work: like the earlier film, it is concerned with a protagonist—or, in this case, two such—at odds with, and at a remove from, community. This sense of separation is again also registered in the way the men on the run are depicted against a daunting landscape that offers little succor and plenty of threat. In fact, it is arguable that the notion of individuals' positioning themselves (or finding themselves positioned) against a social or environmental context in which they have difficulty in realizing security or scope for their own needs—whether seminary or wildly isolated rural settings or the constraints of postwar London or the frozen Arctic—is the most vividly recurring theme in Schepisi's work. As Rennie Ellis wrote: "The theme of the outsider coming to terms with his alienation seems to weave its way through Schepisi's work."[9] The director himself said decades later: "It's been mentioned to me, but I was probably not much aware of it. But there's probably a grain of truth in it, because dealing with outsiders is a great way of dealing with insiders, to see how they react."[10]

Two Men in Flight—From What?

After a panoramic view of mountain scenery ("as enthralling and romantic as a series of Remington paintings," claimed the *Los Angeles Times*),[11] the young Karl Westoff (Gary Busey) emerges from dense foliage. He has accidentally shot a neighbor's son, who was married to his sister Linda (Sharon Compton), and, fleeing into rugged desert country, he meets up with outlaw Barbarosa (Willie Nelson), who has been on the run for thirty years. In a drunken spree on his wedding night to Josephina (Isela Vaga), daughter of the Spanish family, the Zavalas, Barbarosa killed two members of the family and crippled its patriarch, Don Braulio (Gilbert Roland), leaving the latter with one leg. Don Braulio sends his son Eduardo (Danny De La Paz) out to pursue and kill Barbarosa: "Kill him for me, kill him for yourself, kill him for your family," he urges.

Though Barbarosa is the film's eponym, and is played by the revered country singer Willie Nelson, there are really two protagonists in the film, two men in flight from their respective communities. The other is Karl Westoff, a German immigrant farm boy, played by Gary Busey, who had an impressive list of film credits to this point, whereas Nelson's fame rested more on his musical career than on the handful of films he had made by 1982. Though there is just a decade between the two, in William Wittliff's screenplay they emerge more as man and boy, having in common that each has fled family connections after a burst of violence. Texan-born Wittliff had worked with Nelson on *Honeysuckle Rose* (1980), made several films set in his native Texas, and had actually written the screenplay for *Barbarosa* ten years earlier. One reviewer labeled the screenplay "meandering,"[12] and there is some truth to this accusation, especially when one compares it to such common Western motifs as search, fleeing outlaws and emerging communities under pressure. The following study takes on board such thematic issues.

The two men on the run obviously have in common severed family roots and both are outcasts from the vestigial communities they once inhabited, but the film also establishes enough sense of difference in their ways of viewing their experiences to give ballast to the sometimes rambling sense of narrative. As in *Jimmie Blacksmith*, Schepisi never allows interest in characters and the kinds of relationships they form to become subservient to a need for a lot of violent action. The growth of a sort of kinship between the elderly outlaw and the boy who never meant to do anything violent is what matters most, and in the film's last moments Karl arrives dressed as Barbarosa and shoots Eduardo, who is being wreathed for having at last found and killed the outlaw. One Australian critic wrote: "*Barbarosa* is an exquisitely beautiful, hard-cracking portrayal of two men's friendship and hardship in the Texas desert of yesteryear."[13]

It's as though Barbarosa and Karl have finally found common cause, as distinct from that early moment when Karl demurs at the idea of robbing "poor people" whereas Barbarosa claimed, in regard to this, "I have a reputation to maintain 'round here"—i.e., as a bandit, and Wittliff's script is peppered with such touches of humor. In the depiction of the younger man coming to terms with, and in some ways learning from, the aging outlaw, the film inevitably (for me anyway) calls up the gradual rapprochement that sets in between the characters played by Jeffrey Hunter and John Wayne in John Ford's great Western, *The Searchers* (1956). Schepisi is on record as saying, "I'm not a John Ford fan,"[14] but it is at least arguable that, in this central relationship and in the imbuing of the landscape with both grandeur and threat, he often seems to echo the old master. Another echo of Ford is in the racial mix: the Mexican and German in *Barbarosa* reminds one of the Swedish and Indian in the 1956 film. In other words, Schepisi in his first dealings with the American genre has taken on some of its characteristics, whether or not intentionally, and these color our response to *Barbarosa*. There is even an episode set in a Texan cantina, a funeral sequence, and the basic idea of a search (albeit from a different perspective) that are part of the film's texture as they were in *The Searchers*, though it is true that *Barbarosa* does not achieve the thematic resonance of Ford's film, where notions of racism and the idea of home inform its action.

Barbarosa was not a film without its production difficulties for Schepisi. Though he had nothing but praise for Nelson or veteran star Gilbert Roland, he found that Gary Busey, though "a great actor . . . [was] an absolute nightmare to deal with. The art form in that picture was getting Gary out of his motor home and on location so that he could act."[15] Furthermore, there were scheduling problems to do with Busey's and Nelson's availability, and others associated with the location shooting in Texas in the Lajitas area. Schepisi told me that "the transport costs on [the film] were as much as the whole cost of *Jimmie Blacksmith*, and while it was interesting it was very limiting. . . . One of the things we did was to park all our gear and then get smaller trucks to go off to the best place to shoot, leaving the rest of the crew in the original parking spot. So, we sort of worked in the system but found *our* way of doing it."[16] It is only worth quoting this here to stress that Schepisi, gifted as he was in the artistic aspects of filmmaking, was also, perhaps the result of his early start in the business, alert to its logistic challenges, especially now that he found himself in such very different production circumstances in the US. As will become apparent, he adjusted to these with impressive results.

Despite the problems involved in the making and release of his first US film, Schepisi won a fair sample of critical plaudits. Janet Maslin called it "the best western in a long time," with special praise for Ian Baker's photography, which "has a clipped, economical style sometimes given over to sharp surprises, and a boldness befitting the stature that it claims for its hero."[17] In relation to the look of the film's rendering of the Texan landscape, Schepisi told an interviewer: "There are two things I tried to do visually: to show you the beauty of the countryside as it looked to Barbarosa—he stays there because he likes the joint—and to convey the reality beneath the surface, that it's harsh and rocky and thorny, that it hurts."[18] Maslin also opined that "Schepisi's foreignness . . . works to his great advantage . . . [giving] the film's outlaw story its strangeness and beauty."[19] Canby, answering the question posed by the previously quoted title of his review, enthused thus: "Schepisi's *Barbarosa* is so thoroughly entertaining and good-hearted that it comes as something of a shock to realize that it's not only the best Western in years, it's virtually the only Western in years, going on to praise it as being like a timeless country-and-western ballad . . . [that evokes] a vision of the Old West as we like to think it might have been."[20]

ICEMAN (1984)

Another Genre Piece? Yes and No.

In retrospect, it may appear that Schepisi was taking on one US genre after the other. When asked if he had any genre preferences or whether he really preferred the variety, he replied:

> Yes, I'm after variety. I like to go down new roads. Even when I was doing commercials, I liked doing wild things, and the documentaries were very experimental. But with narrative films you have to subdue a lot of that because the story dictates how you are going to tell it: everything's got to be at the service of the story . . . Whatever the genre you've got to find yourself in it; there has to be an element of the personal. . . . Also, when you work in another country, you see things from the outside. You have a different perspective from those on the inside.[21]

He'd begun with the Western, *Barbarosa*, and would later take on comedies and thrillers of various kinds, but he always brought something of his own to bear on the recognizable filmic categories. As noted in relation to *Barbarosa*, he demonstrates again his thematic interest in the plight of the outsider, characteristic of his two Australian features. As Roger Ebert wrote about Schepisi's two preceding films, *Jimmie Blacksmith* and *Barbarosa*: "Both those movies were about men who lived entirely apart from modern society, according to rules of their own.... Now [with *Iceman*] Schepisi has taken that story idea as far as it will go."[22]

Not only are the scientific investigators at a serious physical remove from society, but the eponymous "iceman" can also be seen as an extreme metaphor for the man alone. It is hard to imagine a figure more removed from modern society than a Neanderthal man who emerges fully preserved forty thousand years later from a block of ice, to the amazement of scientists working at an Arctic research station. Yes, *Iceman* belongs firmly in the science-fiction genre but, as I shall argue, it is not constrained by this—and mercifully predated the wildly CGI-dominated examples of the mode in subsequent decades.

Getting Started

Before visual images take over, a poem relating an Inuit legend is given on-screen:

> I, who was born to die,
> Shall live,
> That the world of animals
> And the world of men
> May come together,
> I shall live.

Beginning by quoting this, Schepisi may well be suggesting that *Iceman* will have more on its mind than a conventional sci-fi job, and the film does indeed bear this out. It certainly has some of the expected moments of tension and spectacle that are common to the genre, but it is also intelligently reflective about the phenomenon that sets its narrative in motion.

The film's opening moments in Baker's evocative cinematography depict a vast icy cave, with a helicopter flying above and men walking into the cave. The helicopter flies off with a huge crate, with the camera prowling the icy landscape of rocks and hills, and Bruce Smeaton's eerily haunting music accompanies the flight to a harbor, by which time the figure in the block of ice is becoming clear. A group of scientists at work in the Arctic region has discovered a block of ice from which the Neanderthal man emerges as they carefully chip away the ice with lasers. Pauline Kael, an admirer of Schepisi's films, enthused that "*Iceman* ... begins with perhaps the greatest opening shot I've ever seen: a wide-screen image of Arctic ice and snow, with fluttering helicopters, and the small figures of men moving around a blue-white glacial cave."[23]

Mention of this striking panoramic shot of a Canadian location reminds us that this was Schepisi's most physically demanding production. The ice-bound setting, apart from its physical challenges for cast and crew (and Schepisi actually broke his foot on location), also forced him to alter his shooting style: he and Baker needed a wide lens to capture the icy expanses, as well as their more usual mode of the long lenses to do justice to the faces. While initially thinking that *Iceman* wasn't his "cup of tea," Schepisi took it on because he "thought it could be a thought-provoking but also commercially successful picture, full of pace and energy."[24]

Scientists at Work

There is a persuasive seriousness in the way the scientists go about their work at the research station, believing they have stumbled upon a finding of archaeological and anthropological significance. This is one of the film's strengths, with the scientists behaving convincingly and making contact with their head office via a message sent by cryobiologist Dr. Diane Brady (Lindsay Crouse), who, along with anthropologist Dr. Stephen Shepherd (Timothy Hutton), will be responsible for dealing with the restored Neanderthal man, to be called "Charlie" (John Lone), though the bases for their scientific investigation are markedly different. It is important for the professionalism of the research group to command our attention for the rest of the film's dealings with its stunning discovery.

Schepisi, working from Chris Proser and John Drimmer's screenplay, maintains a compelling sense of speculation and tension by cutting between the faces agog of the watching scientists and the block of ice from which the creature is emerging. What also emerges is the narrative tightener as they wonder if they will be able to reanimate "Charlie" as they work on the body. There are touches of humor in the screenplay, such as when one scientist speculates: "I think he might be conscious but I don't think he's gonna make the Super Bowl." Though Shepherd and Brady will be the key personnel to work with "Charlie," there is also a pervasive sense of a team working in demanding circumstances, and of the moral attitudes the extraordinary discovery enjoins on them.

Brady insists that "Charlie" is "much more than any one man," whereas Shepherd claims "he's a man not a specimen," initiating the narrative hub for the rest of the film, and in doing so will help to account for why *Iceman* is such a rewarding example of its genre. The focus is now firmly on the Neanderthal man, and on what the team will do with him now that they have brought him back to life. They are aware that there are moral as well as scientific issues and responsibilities involved. Shepherd tries to teach "Charlie" to speak English, though this doesn't progress far beyond his throaty efforts to call out "Shepherd," and there is a sort of rapport between the two. Shepherd insists again, "He's not a problem, he's a man," seeking Brady's support and believing a woman might "bring him out of himself." In the end, it might be argued, as Janet Maslin did, that "the caveman . . . somehow brings out their humanity."[25] The claims and aspirations of science and its practitioners are not the only matters of concern: cutting "Charlie" up to see what has made him live so long becomes, for Shepherd especially, less important than understanding him as a human being. In Schepisi's own words, he wanted the film's impression of the Neanderthal "to show some kind of ties between him and us—the spirituality, the beginning of human qualities, the directness of communication. It's a thought-provoker."[26]

How the Film Works

Of course, Schepisi is interested in building up suspense and even some moments of horror, but, unlike a good many more obviously spectacular sci-fi pieces, *Iceman* does also grapple with ideas. Australian critic Evan Williams found it "intelligent and dense with ideas," concluding his review with "as a moral fable it carries a message almost as sad and sobering as [George] Orwell's."[27] In doing so, Schepisi gives the film a richer texture than mere concentration on visual effect or narrative action might have achieved. For instance, the film seems to ask such questions as to whether science is above criticism and whether other things matter too, possibly even more. In raising such matters non-didactically, the film is indebted to two very engaging performances from Timothy Hutton and Lindsay Crouse as dedicated researchers and decent human beings. Further, there is a masterly melding of the grotesque and the humanly touching in Chinese American John Lone's rendering of "Charlie," that prisoner of time whose fate we are made to care about. Lone's performance received virtually unanimous critical praise, along the lines of "a beautifully conceived central performance"[28] and "Lone handles the difficult role with great skill."[29]

As in his two preceding films, Schepisi has exhibited a sympathetic concern for the outsider's situation, which is presented in its most extreme form here. However, if those two earlier films had their production problems, these were slight in comparison to what Schepisi had to deal with in making *Iceman*. Some of the interiors were built in Vancouver, but much of it was also shot in and around Churchill, in the far north of Manitoba, in freezing conditions, and there was the matter of building a $500,000 vivarium, an enormous hollow full of cliffs and caves to simulate the Neanderthal's natural environment. Interviewer James Verniere is no doubt right when he describes *Iceman* as "logistically . . . Schepisi's most arduous film," adding that it required five helicopters to ferry filmmakers to the ice-bound locations, which placed serious pressure on the number of shots to be achieved each day.[30]

Following *Barbarosa*, several projects had fallen through for Schepisi by the time he began work on *Iceman*. As one who is not a serious sci-fi fan, I can only say that *Iceman* emerges as an engrossing piece of work that warrants Roger Ebert's accolade: "This movie is spellbinding storytelling. It begins with such a simple premise and creates such a genuinely intriguing situation that we're not just entertained, we're drawn into the argument."[31]

PLENTY (1985)

By the time Schepisi came to filming *Plenty*, he had made the above two US genre pieces—*Barbarosa* and *Iceman*—and his business acumen as well as his directorial skills had established themselves outside his native Australia. In spite of the Internet Movie Database's listing the film as UK/US[32], *Plenty* is, in terms of its production source, entirely a US project, as the more reliable *Monthly Film Bulletin* noted in its review.[33] Given IMDb's listing as a co-production, it nevertheless goes on to record, as the film's opening credits do, that *Plenty* is "An RKO Presentation" and "An Edward R. Pressman Production"—with the further on-screen title "A Fred Schepisi Film." Nevertheless, it feels more like a British film: it was largely set (and shot) in England, with forays into France, Belgium, and Jordan, and most of its personnel are either British or Australian.

So, Schepisi was now an international director, though as we shall see, wherever his films are made or set, there are continuing thematic patterns (and some narrative practices) that clearly contribute to his directorial signature. Not that he would describe himself as an auteur, but, when one turns to *Plenty*, there is that recurring interest in the way he chooses to locate one person's complex story against the background of a changing world. Think, for instance, of Jimmie Blacksmith's search for identity while Australia's states are embracing the idea of Federation.

Whose Film?

It is one thing, though, to talk of "A Fred Schepisi Film," but another to consider the key collaborators who made *Plenty* the absorbing experience that it became. In the end, it will be Schepisi who is responsible for orchestrating all the other creative inputs, but two others who stand out are obviously David Hare and Meryl Streep.

Schepisi's filmography is rich in adaptations of works of literature and theatre, and he has a record of working with the antecedent authors in the process, even when the latter do not always seek on-screen credit for their contribution, as was the case on *Jimmie Blacksmith*. On *Plenty*, however, playwright David Hare has sole credit for the screenplay for the film derived from his play. By coincidence, the filming of *Plenty* was no sooner underway than Hare, one of the most critically acclaimed playwrights of the later twentieth century, got the chance to direct his first film, *Wetherby* (1985), which, like *Plenty*, also draws parallels between private life and the public domain.

With regard to *Plenty* and his function as screenwriter, Hare is on record as saying: "I adapted the play myself. . . . I had taken out an awful lot of words in a quite simple-minded way as an attempt to make it more of a narrative, and both Meryl Streep and Fred Schepisi said that what actually distinguishes *Plenty* is what the characters say, so they put a lot of the words back in again."[34] For his part, in a later interview Schepisi said: "I shocked David by insisting he put more and more dialogue back in the film."[35] Closer analysis of the film will explore whether the resulting screenplay is wordier, maybe spelling out key notions more explicitly than is needed. Assessing the adaptation of plays to screen is always a trickier undertaking than is discussion of the ties that bind novel and film. The latter pair are *texts*, more or less permanently available in identical replications. So too are play and film, if by "play," we limit ourselves to the idea of the playwright's script, usually in book form, but, in doing so, we are aware of a crucial absence: that is, the performance of the play, which was presumably the playwright's goal.

As a play, *Plenty* unfolded in twelve quite short scenes, beginning in London in 1962, then in Scene 2 reverting to wartime France, then to postwar London from 1947 to Easter 1962, followed by a brief interlude in a Blackpool hotel in June 1962, and finally a sort of epilogue set in the French countryside at the end of World War II. In Hare's own words when he was interviewed at the time of the film adaptation: "On stage *Plenty* was organised by scene and focused on the development of a character. On film, we had the chance for much more narrative drive and could show a lot of history."[36] He was, however, very satisfied to have Schepisi as director, and was quoted as saying: "He is a wonderful pictorial film maker, and I felt his style would go well with such a literary subject. The balance would be very good."[37] As we shall see later, not every critic would agree. It is at least arguable that the film's "narrative drive" is compromised by its sometimes disconcerting jumps in time and place, though one writer praised it as "a beautiful movie—great to look at and so well-crafted—with the demanding David Hare play all straightened out and told in proper sequence."[38]

Are we really shown, as Hare claimed above, "a lot of history," or just a selective rendering of what bears on Susan Traherne's fate?

The answer to the latter may well be that it is characteristic of many Schepisi films to filter wider social issues through individual lives. And whereas a realistic sitting-room setting for a play may stand for a whole house, even for a particular neighborhood, film (like the novel) is more advantageously placed to offer us the illusion of a whole created world. This is not to make evaluative judgment between the two modes, but simply to draw attention to what the filmmaker Hare has achieved in broadening the scope of the action that various other collaborators will access to give us that sense of the wider world. Through its mise-en-scène, *Plenty* acquires a detailed photographic realism that goes beyond setting, rendered through choices made about lighting, camera movement and angle, editing procedures, and soundtrack. In the end, these are the choices Schepisi as director has made and activated via such valued colleagues as cinematographer Baker and music director Smeaton.

As for the third name adduced under the question "whose film?" we should not underestimate the importance of its star, Meryl Streep. I refer here not just to how, as protagonist in the film's action (to which I shall return), she will govern so much of the viewer's response to the film, but also to her function in the setting up of the film in the first place. With her participation, *Plenty* became a different order of film. She was, as they say, "hot" in industry terms. The stage play, first performed at London's National Theatre in 1978, had starred Kate Nelligan when it appeared on Broadway in 1983. She was Tony-nominated for her performance and was a much respected name in the theatre but not one much known to cinemagoers in 1985. This was no doubt a matter of concern to the film's co-producers, Edward R. Pressman and Joe Papp, in securing the film's financing.

Schepisi, speaking of the decision to cast Streep, felt it "finally boiled down to financial considerations. If we went with Kate, we would get $7m and no guarantee that the picture would ever be made. If we went with Meryl, we'd get $10m."[39] Streep's bankability as a *film* star enabled the film to get off the ground industrially, to which Schepisi attested in a later interview: "It was still terribly difficult to get the money . . . but Meryl [is] clearly the premier actress of her generation on film"[40]—and has probably maintained that status over the intervening decades. In the early 1980s, Streep had been seen in an English role in Karel Reisz's *The French Lieutenant's Woman* (1981), so that not only would her name carry the necessary weight in the US but she had also been widely accepted by UK audiences when playing one of their own. In a still later interview, Schepisi spoke of the need to cast the other important roles in the film with actors "who had already achieved a certain amount of notoriety so they wouldn't be fazed acting opposite Meryl Streep."[41] (With names such as John Gielgud and Ian McKellen, he was on safe ground here.) She was not only responsible for the film's funding but her dealings with the pressures on her character's inner life also provide the core element in the film's narrative course.

So, while *Plenty* is technically a US film, when we answer the question "whose film?" we have to take into account an English playwright and screenwriter, an Australian director (along with several of his key associates, such as Smeaton and Baker), and a top-flight US star. Given that the film is largely set, as noted above, in England, it is worth noting that this may have been Schepisi's first entirely international film, but we should never underestimate where the production money has come from and the potential influence of this factor on the final production.

Towards the End of the War

Hare's screenplay, unlike his theatre piece, opens behind enemy lines in France during the latter stages of World War II, when Susan Traherne, an upper-class Englishwoman, is working for the Special Operations Executive. In a dimly lit forest, she and others are looking up at the sound of an aircraft, from which parachutists descend. One of these is Lazar (Sam Neill), at whom Susan at first points a gun, before he says, "*Je peux tout expliquer*," after which they walk off to her quarters in the neighboring village, where they embark on a brief affair. She weeps: "I'm so frightened . . . I don't want to die," and he comforts her. The war setting for this opening enjoins on them, as enacted by Streep and Neill, a convincing sexual urgency, which will not be notably apparent in Susan's subsequent life in postwar England.

The wartime images of the village—with German soldiers patrolling—contrast with the intimacy of Susan's apartment, and these and the long shots of the castle-like structure on the side of a hill, on which the village is set, remind us that place always matters to Schepisi. As he once claimed: "Where things are said becomes as important as what is being said. The locations are a genuine character in the film."[42] There will be telling close-ups of the protagonists, particularly of Susan, but he regularly ensures that we consider what these tell us in relation to the larger setting, both physical and social. He eschews gratuitous pictorialism while making place *work*: when Susan and Lazar admire a "mackerel sky" from their window, this image will find its echo towards the end of the film. So, too, will the close-up of the cufflinks he leaves behind in her flat, she having gone to her workplace in the village, when they have a coincidental re-meeting in the film's penultimate scene. Set in a bleakly isolated-seeming seaside hotel, its façade seems a metaphor for a nation in stasis.

Susan is not presented as a stoical heroine. She cowers in fear as Germans ride by in jeeps and there is a touch of poignancy as she watches Lazar ride out of her life. A good deal is established in these opening scenes about the kind of woman she is—at least how she is in a time and place of war. There isn't space to discuss every episode of the film in this kind of detail, but it is essentially through her responses that the changing world of war and its aftermath is rendered. The fleeting nature of wartime meetings is reinforced by the following scene in Brussels, where diplomat Raymond Brock (Charles Dance) and the British ambassador, Sir Leonard Darwin (John Gielgud), seek to console her about the death of her "husband," Tony, and to discuss what she would have them do with his body. She explains that she wasn't Tony's wife: "In fact, I was barely his mistress." Nonetheless, she explains that conditions of war had made the deception necessary. Sir Leonard now talks of "reconstruction" and how there are "lots to get on with." That is, we are now being ushered into the world of post-war England, and the kind of life this will open up for Susan.

Susan and the Post-War World

Matters of class and social/political change as epitomized in Susan's life in the decades following World War II provide the context for the drama of most of the rest of the film. Schepisi, as an Australian, aware of the influence of elements of the British class system, registered how "crippling" he found it in England. "'Crippling' for the English," he emphasized, "I wasn't going to let it cripple me."[43] In this, he is part of the tradition of filmmakers from other countries directing their attention to the mores of, say, the US or Britain, as several of Schepisi's Australian contemporaries, such as Peter Weir or Bruce Beresford, had done. What is being suggested is that a director with no place in the British class structure may have been able to view it more dispassionately.

Certainly, there had been some relaxing of the class barriers during the war and, in *Plenty*, Susan's experiences offer a clear picture of this in the twenty years following, while still aware of how the old order could continue to reassert itself. Back in England and living with the very upper-class Brock, she makes friends with the outgoing Alice Park (Tracey Ullman), who moves in much racier circles than Susan has been used to. There are images of postwar austerity certainly, with some grim-looking shots of bomb-damaged streets, but there is also an air of a new liveliness in pub scenes, where Brock tends to look uncomfortable, a very noisy jazz cellar or a Chinese restaurant, where Brock is uneasy about the food. In his rather stiff response to the changing scene, he embodies some of the film's criticism of the class system, whereas Susan, bored with her job in a shipyard office, claims, "I want to change everything and I don't know how," and calls Brock's boss, Darwin, "a buffoon," to which Brock replies: "Darwin just has a problem adjusting to the modern age."

Susan gets a job with the committee in charge of the coronation celebrations in 1953, a link with the ongoing hierarchy of the land, but, having broken with Brock, she starts an affair with Mick (Sting), one of Alice's working-class friends, by whom she wants to have a child. This venture fails and she will reject him, but again the sense of class barriers no longer being as obstructive as once they were is part of the film's fabric, and Schepisi, working from Hare's screenplay (on which he made uncredited suggestions), renders a potent sense of a nation in a state of change. In this matter, the following comment by one reviewer seems to me unduly severe: "The film's perspective on postwar Britain ... is too broad and partial to be convincing."[44] This seems to miss the point that *Plenty* is not "history" but essentially one woman's perception of, and response to, the changing times. The ultimate event in the depiction of British political decline comes with the Suez crisis, in which the West tried to regain control of the Canal, and this is contemplated along with Susan's disintegration. Following a nervous breakdown, she has married Brock, become a society hostess at one of whose dinner parties she pours scorn on Darwin, unaware that he has resigned over what he saw as Britain's shameless role in the crisis.

Streep's sure grasp of the character of Susan is the lifeline that holds together the film's vision of a world in both recovery and decline. Her wartime courage and the sense of doing important work do not find the same scope in the postwar world. In this respect, *Plenty* may be seen as having some continuity with Schepisi's two major Australian films to this point: *The Devil's Playground* (1976) and *The Chant of Jimmie Blacksmith* (1978). All three are concerned with the failure of the societies they depict—the Jesuit seminary, pre-Federation Australia, and postwar Britain—to offer appropriate sustenance to one of their more sensitive members. In fact, Streep seems often to have been acting out the role of a woman caught between untenable options, in such diverse films as *Kramer vs. Kramer* (1979) and *Sophie's Choice* (1982), and *Plenty* requires of her a deepening sense of Susan's being at odds with the world she was once used to. Whereas war had made its own demands, in the succeeding decades she has had to struggle to find acceptable roles and places in which to feel calmly at one with herself—and she is struggling to do so in a country that seems to be in decline.

In Streep's performance, she, like the film at large, is brilliantly supported by the likes of Ruth Myers, the costume designer, and J. Roy Helland, responsible for her hair and makeup. Their contributions collude with Streep's gifts for changing facial expression to create moments of social poise or mental unease or wild anger, just as, say, Richard Macdonald's production design and Ian Baker's camera incarnate the changing surfaces of British life in the relevant decades. As one critic wrote: "Schepisi makes every stately London building and street lean in and squeeze his heroine,"[45] and by "Schepisi" is implied the contributions of those other collaborators. Susan's story is not a mere allegory of the nation's fortunes but, as she approaches the violent end of her marriage with Brock and Britain stumbles into the Suez crisis, the film compels us to think of the two collapses—the individual and the national—in a sort of uneasy and complex tandem. Seeming to miss this key thematic and structural point, Vincent Canby, in a rather vicious review, dismissed it (and the play) as "a muddled attempt to equate the emotional longueurs of Susan Traherne with life in post-war Britain"![46] It is truer to view Susan's dispiriting experience of postwar life as an "anticlimax after the idealism and excitements of wartime," as a more positive review put it.[47]

The film's last moments return Susan to the time and scene of its opening. She is on a hillside in France, this time in sunshine, where she talks with a farmer about how different life will be now that the war has been won, and about the English and "feelings": "Things will quickly change. We have grown up.... There will be days and days and days like this." This visually idyllic vista and Susan's effortless optimism provide in hindsight the most poignant appraisal of all that has gone before.

Schepisi has said that "in *Plenty* there's a repetition of images so that you're constantly introducing new places in exactly the same way."[48] Take the scene in which Susan, aware that her breakdown has damaged Brock's diplomatic career, intercedes on his behalf with his chilly superior, Sir Andrew Charleston (Ian McKellen), the camera steadily held on the two. One reviewer, otherwise not especially enthusiastic about the film, felt that this "brilliant scene says more than the whole of the rest of the film about Great Britain in the dying days of empire."[49] This resonates with her earlier exchanges with the British Ambassador, or the dinner at which she harangues the guests. One also recalls Susan's French workplace, where she had serious matters to attend to, when she is shown bored in her postwar job in England. But nothing is more pertinent to the film's overall emotional and thematic content than that final image of what was expected but did not happen. There may be moments when important matters of class or politics are spelled out more explicitly than needed, but Schepisi's real achievement is in the melding of word and image in depicting the challenges and conflicts that beset individuals and a nation trying to find their way in a peacetime of changing signposts.

ROXANNE (1987)

Roxanne was Schepisi's last US-shot film, after making *Plenty* in the UK, before returning to Australia to make *Evil Angels* (US title, *A Cry in the Dark*). While in the US during the first half of the 1980s, he had broadened his genre range and adjusted to different filmmaking practices in a country where filmmaking was a more firmly organized and controlled business than he had previously found it to be in Australia. One of its enduring characteristics was the established genre categories that were part of its prolific output. As Schepisi himself said: "I never wanted to be repeating what I'd done. To get to do comedy was difficult because no one believed I could do it because of the films I'd already done."[50] *Roxanne* was his first venture into the comedy genre. There had of course been some humorous moments in films as diverse as *The Devil's Playground*, *Iceman*, and *Plenty*, but *Roxanne* was his generic breakthrough in the matter of comedy. Not that it had been easy to achieve this: he had worked on several comedy screenplays that he failed to get made, and there were two by screenwriter Steve Tesich that Schepisi liked: "Both comedies of tone and character. They were very funny, but I couldn't get anywhere with them."[51] He must have been cheered when David Denby wrote: "*Roxanne*, directed by Fred Schepisi, is a lovely movie, one of the rare American comedies that depend on feelings more than gags."[52]

There is nevertheless some sense of continuity with his earlier work. For instance, he is again attracted to the idea of a protagonist who is to some extent set apart from his colleagues or friends, even if this does not lead to the same degree of "outsider" status, with fire chief protagonist C. D. Bales. C. D. (Steve Martin) is aware that his outsize nose cannot but attract attention. Also, his new colleague, Chris (Rick Rossovich), has the handsome looks that draw "chicks," as someone tells him, but is shy to the point of inarticulateness in the company of women.

While not setting out to make an airtight case for Schepisi as auteur, I would also note his readiness to take on extended location filming, as well as recurring thematic and artistic preoccupations. In his Australian films to this point, he chose for *The Devil's Playground* a country house and surrounds away from Melbourne and outback

New South Wales for *Jimmie Blacksmith*. His first two US films were at least as remotely filmed: *Barbarosa* in Texas and *Iceman* in Manitoba and British Columbia; and now *Roxanne* was filmed entirely in British Columbian sites, including Nelson, the setting for much of the film's action. Location clearly matters significantly to Schepisi's filming, even when it involves considerable difficulties. It is as though his protagonists can only be fully understood in relation to the places where they are located—and often from which they feel in some measure dissociated. As one critic observed, in relation to the thematic or technical levels of Schepisi's films: "[His] visual style is unmistakable, and his interest in individuals facing off against a hostile world has been consistent across a wide range of genres," including his first three US films.[53]

Adaptation from Rostand to Schepisi

As in the case of *Jimmie Blacksmith* and in such subsequent films as *Plenty, Six Degrees of Separation, Last Orders*, and *Eye of the Storm*, he was interested in the processes of adaptation and worked closely with either the author or the screenwriter or both in effecting the transfer to the screen. In his own words regarding adaptation: "You should 'play around' as far as you're interpreting the work as a film project, while doing justice to the original work. I think if you're taking on someone's work and you're going to turn it into a film, you owe it to them not just to use it as a springboard for your own shit. If you want to do that, write your own."[54] When it comes to *Roxanne*, Schepisi is one of several dozen filmmakers of large and small screens who have adapted Edmond Rostand's play *Cyrano de Bergerac*. Operatic and ballet versions of the play have also been committed to film. Probably the best-known feature films derived from Rostand's dealings with human emotions and difficulties are Michael Gordon's 1950 version, with José Ferrer's Oscar-winning performance, and Jean-Paul Rappeneau's 1990 version, with Oscar-nominated Gérard Depardieu in the title role. The mere retention of Rostand's title suggests that it has assumed almost mythic status for its depiction of love's possibilities. Roger Ebert's review of the film suggested that the "play that was written in 1890 . . . still strikes some kind of universal note, maybe because for all of us there is some attribute or appendage we secretly fear people will ridicule."[55]

Schepisi's *Roxanne* is a contemporary American take on the famous original, working from a screenplay by, and starring, comedian Steve Martin, who was also executive producer on the film. This time the Cyrano protagonist is small-town fire chief C. D. Bales ("Charlie" to friends), not so much a swordsman as a wordsman while still hewing to the play's central idea: that is, it is still the story of the guy with the huge nose that gets in the way of activities such as drinking and kissing but with a gift for words with which he helps the handsome, bumbling colleague to woo the object of his affections.

Schepisi and Martin—on the Nose

The nose is probably what is most adhesively associated with Rostand's eponym and one of the film's smartest moves is in the way it builds up to the first profile of C. D. Bales. Walking with a tennis racquet, he is first seen reprimanding two sauntering lads who mock his nose, so he kicks them and then flattens them both, as if playing tennis (he announces the score as "15 love"). All of this is executed, via Ian Baker's judicious camerawork, from angles that preclude a side view of the crucial proboscis. When, at the episode's end, a close-up profile reveals its dimensions, we are left to reflect on what to assume about C. D. Is his rough treatment of the two lads meant to be a legitimate reaction to what may well have been a lifetime of mockery? Very soon, though, the film assures us that we are not meant to be solemn about this.

Two newcomers to Nelson will have significant bearing on C. D.'s life there—and on the significance of his nose. He meets beautiful astronomer, the eponymous Roxanne (Daryl Hannah), when she inadvertently locks herself out of her house while naked. He comes to her rescue, albeit clumsily, and falls for her, but is too self-conscious about his nasal excess to pursue her further. The other newcomer is the hunky Chris, the latest addition to the fire department, who also falls for Roxanne but is too shy and verbally inept to make any progress in relation to her.

The gist of the film's narrative—and the source of some of its funniest moments—is in the way this trio's connections will be sorted.

Chris's inarticulateness in the presence of women who may care for his looks means that he is not getting anywhere with Roxanne, until C. D., revealing generosity, prepares the words for him when Chris writes letters to Roxanne and, later, outside her window is prompted by the hidden C. D. to utter words of romantic passion that lead him to her bed. Chris is apt to talk grossly about her body and, in a rare perceptive moment, he later confides to C. D.: "She wants someone who looks like me and talks like you." This key to the two "defects"— grotesque nose and verbal incompetence, both obstacles to their success with women—gives the film a sturdy structure.

The preceding account doesn't really do justice to the film as comedy, though, like all the best comedies, *Roxanne* has its serious resonances. Nevertheless, the whole business of Chris's wooing of Roxanne through C. D.'s words, whether in writing or in speech prompted by radio connection, is written and played for well-earned laughter. For instance, in one episode Chris turns up for a meeting with Roxanne wearing a bizarre cap with earflaps to conceal the earphones that connect him via short-wave radio to C. D. in the latter's fire truck. C. D.'s poetic words are several times interrupted by official messages for the fire department, along the lines of "Car 3 proceed to 279." When at her bidding, Chris uses his own words and starts talking of her breasts ("like melons"), prompting her to run inside.

There is plenty of verbal inventiveness elsewhere in the film, as in the barroom scene in which a bullying guy taunts C. D., calling him "big nose" for all the crowd to hear. C. D. will knock the guy down, but before doing so, has the crowd hooting with laughter as he delivers twenty much funnier insults about nose-size: "Laugh and the world laughs with you; sneeze and it's, 'Goodbye Seattle'" or "Would you mind not bobbing your head, the orchestra keeps changing its tempo" or "The paranoid yelling 'Keep that guy away from my cocaine.'" It is a smart script that can keep this up for twenty such one-liners and keep C. D. likable—and obviously liked by the roomful of locals.

However, the film's comedy is not just verbal; there are some joyously physical, visual moments. These can be personal and nose-related, as when C. D. has to ask for a straw to drink wine, and episodes in which the incompetent firemen are trained in hosing to the tune of "The Blue Danube," as C. D. dances around the tangling hose. But Steve Martin's screenplay and the emphases in Schepisi's direction show, without the least didacticism, the kinds of limitations to which human lives can be subject. There is even an overweight boy on a rooftop who won't come down because "kids call me 'Porky' at school," until C. D. goes up to comfort him. This brief moment is done without sentimentality and works as another small reminder of the way "difference" can affect, even perhaps shape, a life. As Roger Ebert wrote at the time of the film's release: "Inside every adult is a second-grader still terrified of being laughed at," and in this matter, the film registers heart as well as wit.[56]

Schepisi would make several more comedies in the US in the 1990s, but, arguably, *Roxanne* is his most fully achieved contribution to the genre. Working from Martin's screenplay, Schepisi draws very likable performances from Martin, Hannah, and Rossovich, as well as with other more fleeting roles, like the gaggle of older women anxious to get home in time for *Dallas*. The director also maintains a tonal control that never loses a sense of things that matter lurking beneath the liveliest comic invention.

Roxanne followed a disappointing period for Schepisi when several proposals failed to materialize, and he later claimed that: "*Roxanne* was a great experience for me and a breakthrough."[57] It was also the first box-office success of his US career: "*Roxanne* made money. More than that, it was funny and warm. It could have been just a conventional comedy, but it became more than that. It made the studios appreciate my skills more, and it also made money. I am not sure in which order that goes, but I have an idea."[58]

Though the *Village Voice* reviewer deemed it "merely anemic," claiming that, "in his weakest outing yet, Schepisi shows a negative flair for comedy,"[59] the film won critical plaudits on each side of the Atlantic. The *Washington Post* declared that it was "the most unabashed, and most satisfying, romantic movie to come along in years. It's a swooning, delicate, heart-on-its-sleeve work. And so fulsome is its tenderness and naiveté that it requires a leap of imagination from the viewer to get on its wavelength."[60] Denby, quoted above, summed up with: "[Schepisi has] created a genial, relaxed, and expansive movie."[61] In the UK, Kim Newman wrote: "*Roxanne*, Fred Schepisi's least personal work, emerges as his best film.... It manages to charm and amuse, and Schepisi is to be commended for applying a hitherto unsuspected light touch."[62] It was certainly very different in tone from the film that took him back to Australia in the following year, but it had helped to establish him as a director whose thematic interests and technical accomplishment could make themselves felt across a wider generic range than had previously been expected.

Chapter Five

SCHEPISI AND THE CHAMBERLAIN AFFAIR— *A CRY IN THE DARK*

Having established himself both as a director of some standing, at home and abroad, and as one adroit at adjusting himself to a range of genres, Schepisi was urged by the English producer Verity Lambert to return to Australia for his next venture. This was to be *Evil Angels* (released in the US as *A Cry in the Dark*), derived from author John Bryson's novel,[1] which was in turn based on what was perhaps the most sensational "murder" case in Australian history. It will become apparent why "murder" is given in quotation marks.

THE CHAMBERLAIN AFFAIR

The "Chamberlain affair," as it is widely remembered, involved the death of a baby reputedly stolen from a tent in the Northern Territory tourist area of Ayers Rock (now known by its native name, Uluru). Michael and Lindy Chamberlain, a Seventh Day Adventist pastor and his wife, with their three children, were holidaying there, when at night Lindy heard a baby cry and found her baby daughter, Azaria, missing from its basket in the tent. She claimed to have seen a dingo leaving the tent, carrying something in its mouth. Search parties were unable to find the baby's body. After two inquests in Alice Springs, which supported the Chamberlains' claims, they were brought to a trial in Darwin after further investigation. As a result, in October 1982 Lindy was charged with murder and sentenced to life imprisonment, and Michael, as accessory, to eighteen months, but his sentence was suspended in the interests of caring for his two remaining children.

When a further article of the baby's clothing bearing dingo hairs was found in 1986, Lindy was declared innocent and released from prison, and all charges against the Chamberlains were dropped. In the history of real-life Australian judicial dramas, few can have created such a media frenzy or roused such public feeling, whether opprobrious or outraged for what some felt was a cruel decision. The death of the child Azaria Chamberlain, allegedly murdered by her mother in outback Australia, divided public opinion in a sensational manner. There was some feeling that Lindy Chamberlain's seeming composure in the courtrooms was not what would have been expected of a grieving mother, and the newspapers and television were unrelenting in their pursuit of the case. The media were after "stories" rather than facts, seeking readers and viewers, rather than measured, responsible accounts of a terrible incident. In one lawyer's terse summary, quoted by Bryson, "the newspapers were in the pursuit of sales rather than justice."[2] Or as Paul Everingham, the chief minister of the Northern Territory at the time said on radio: "The media's acting like a buncha vampires."[3]

JOHN BRYSON'S BOOK

The Chamberlain affair has prompted a great deal of writing, not just in the voracious media but also in book-length studies with titles such as *Azaria: The Trial of the Century*[4] and *The Azaria Mystery: A Reason to Kill*.[5] The publication details can now seem vague in relation to the twenty books inspired by the case, so it is possible that some were self-published, but, even if so, this does not diminish the enormous interest the case aroused. The most significant book-length study (and at 563 pages, the length is impressive) was John Bryson's *Evil Angels*, or as it came to be called in the US, the UK, and several other countries, *A Cry in the Dark*), and Fred Schepisi's film would draw heavily on Bryson's account when he came to make the film.

Bryson's book is presented as a novel, but it obviously draws on a huge range of information from many researchers and newspapers and other sources. It may perhaps come under the now-frequent heading of "creative nonfiction," but, however one characterizes it, Schepisi clearly drew significantly on it when he came to make his film. The book is certainly based on the welter of public and other knowledge, and it just as surely involves a massive imaginative grasp that welds this into a coherent narrative whole. However, though allowing that the "book shows you how a lot of things were colored by the media," he also claimed that "it doesn't tell you, and it doesn't purport to tell you, anything about the Chamberlains."[6] On reading the book, I am inclined to dispute this, but Schepisi goes on to give the rationale for his film: "The film is the book *and* the private lives of the Chamberlains."[7] A study of the film will support the latter claim but without necessarily dismissing the earlier one.

GETTING THE FILM STARTED

By the time he turned to filming *Evil Angels*, Schepisi had had experience in adapting a highly regarded novel (*Jimmie Blacksmith*) and a play (*Plenty*) by one of the respected playwrights of the day, as well as a wittily reimagined version of a classic French play (*Roxanne*). Now, he was faced not merely with making a film from a novel of the same name but adapting real-life events with all their terrible repercussions. Here are his own words as he embarked on this formidable project that had brought him back to Australia:

> The novel was pretty much about the facts and the court case and we added a good deal. It was a big worry to me and I wasn't going to do the project, but the English producer Verity Lambert kept driving me nuts. Finally one day she rang me and said: "I know why you're not doing this.... You don't know how to." So, I said, "Right," because there was a script and it was pretty straightforward, and I went away and worked on it a bit, then rang her back and said: "Here's how you do it." Two weeks later I had a phone call from her: "I've got someone to talk to you" and the someone was Meryl Streep.[8]

For Schepisi, having worked so successfully with Streep on *Plenty*, the mention of her name may well have been the deciding factor in his committing to the film.

Though bearing the credit "A Golan-Globus Production [US], in association with Cinema Verity [UK]," *Evil Angels* was essentially Australian-made, filmed entirely in Australia, much of it on location in the north. As the end credits note, it was "Filmed at Australian Film Studios, Dallas," an outer Melbourne suburb (i.e., apart from location work), and was "Developed with financial assistance from the Australian Film Commission." David Stratton reported that "it became the biggest production ever undertaken in Australia ... [with locations] thousands of miles apart, the speaking cast numbered 350 and there were nearly 4000 extras in all."[9] Obviously, it was going to be a difficult and expensive production that might well need a star name to get it started, and then to sell it.

With Streep interested, Schepisi took another look at the project, and, he says, found another way of doing it. "What it is about, basically, is the public perception and the private reality. The whole film is about that, and the whole structure is about that."[10] With this in mind, he, Streep, and Sam Neill (who would play Michael Chamberlain, and with whom Schepisi had also worked on *Plenty*) spent some time talking to the Chamberlains, and the resulting film testifies to Schepisi's formulation about the public/private dichotomy and interaction. Bringing in the Chamberlains was important to the whole enterprise. As quoted above, Schepisi claimed that Bryson's book "doesn't tell you ... anything about the Chamberlains ... but I believed the Chamberlains had to be in the film."[11] As Stratton wrote, "Initially the Chamberlains themselves were nervous about the prospect of a film being made about them," but, after screenwriter Robert Caswell spent time with them, Stratton quoted Schepisi as saying: "They realised we didn't want to sensationalise, but to present the facts as accurately as we could."[12]

In some ways, then, *Evil Angels* was his most challenging film to date. It was important to him that all those involved in its making should remain nonjudgmental about its subject matter, which was still—and to this day remains—controversial: "This story involves a whole country, behaving like idiots."[13] In a sense, he was playing with a fire not wholly extinguished and, though the Chamberlains stand at its center, the surrounding drama of how the nation, fed relentlessly by the media, responded to it would be as crucial to the film's thematic interests and structural procedures—and, as will become clear, to its visual character. As to the latter, he was aiming at what he described as a "home-movie style"[14] to embrace the foregoing concepts.

STRUCTURING THE "FACTS"

It was no doubt plain to Schepisi from the start that the film couldn't just trawl through the events of the case as so many of the newspaper accounts did, hitting on, whenever possible, a new sensational development. Or, one might add, as Lindy Chamberlain does in Bryson's book, when she is being interviewed by police some time after the event, and when she "might stray about between the ramshackle details in her memory."[15] Her attempt at reconstructing the order of the happenings at Ayers Rock is most likely the way it was in reality, but the film has to work at shaping the lead-up to the "murder" (if that is what it was), its activation and aftermath, in a manner that will exert a dramatic hold on the material—and on the potential audiences. In a two-hour film there will be limits to how much screen time can be allowed to the ramblings of what one investigator considers "their quite imperfect story."[16] The deficiencies and inconsistencies have to be rendered as central to the case: Schepisi's challenge was to do so in cinematic terms.

The film has to interest us in the Chamberlains from the outset, and the screenplay (co-written by Schepisi and Robert Caswell) introduces them in a voice-over that announces: "Our pastor Michael and his wife Lindy stand before you today with their boys, Aiden and Reagan, and their new little daughter and baby sister, Azaria Chantel Loren Chamberlain." This is being spoken to the congregation in the Seventh Day Adventist church of Mt. Isa. The Chamberlains are established as a loving family unit against a background of their strong religious affiliation, both of which elements will prove crucial and be subject to intense pressure in the ensuing months.

The camera cuts from the church congregation to the noise of an approaching truck, the driver of which makes a crude remark to his mate as they pass the church: "Take a look at those fucking Adventists." This comment anticipates the sort of brutal responses that will be the Chamberlains' lot in the years ahead. The settled family and the idea of threats that would *un*settle it have been articulated when the film is only a few minutes old. When talking to the couple after the film was shown, Schepisi found that they "had no idea of the scale of the thing, of what was against them."[17] Considered in hindsight, the film's opening images—the long shot of a rocky outcrop, then straggling towns and mountains, followed by the church and the abusive driver—have done an apt job in setting the film's narrative in motion and foreshadowing its visual power.

HOW DOES THE STORY UNFOLD?

Though the film will have to cut again and again between the private and the public, between individuals and baying crowds, between times and places—and much of its fluency will depend on editor Jill Bilcock's adeptness in the creation of telling juxtapositions and requires a basic, underlying structure to bind it together persuasively. To this end, the film bookends the tragic death of Azaria and the ensuing investigation with the personal story of the Chamberlain family. It begins and ends with the family in the setting of the church and, throughout, the relationship between Lindy and Michael is dramatized as a marriage under exceptional strain, a strain from which their religious beliefs seem barely able to protect them.

The narrative arc of *Evil Angels* is partly—possibly even essentially—determined by known information in relation to the most sensational case in Australian legal history, but this must also be shaped for the film. Opening on the family unit in the setting of its religious beliefs, followed by the image of Lindy sewing a dress for Azaria and happily preparing for the holiday in central Australia, lays a basis for the tumultuous upheaval that the lives introduced will undergo.

The notion of the holiday as a family occasion is clinched in the shot in which Michael shows the boys on a large map where they are headed. During this brief episode, the older son makes a remark that, in hindsight at least, will resonate in the film: "Daddy had wanted to go further north where they have the biggest barramundi in the world—but Mummy had other plans." This sounds like a jokey quip, but, in its suggestion that the parents are not always in agreement, it anticipates their later serious disagreements after the first day of the court case. It also draws fleeting attention to the fact that it was Lindy who wanted to go to Ayers Rock camp site, rather than up north, and, that if they had followed Michael's wishes, Azaria's death would not have happened.

The foregoing is not to overemphasize the importance of a brief moment but, rather, to suggest that in the unfolding of the narrative nothing is without function, nothing is wasted. Via some of Ian Baker's most ravishing cinematography and Bilcock's astute editing, the film cuts from this domestic scene to a long shot of Ayers Rock, the site of the ensuing tragedy. At this early point, the family is then seen climbing about the Rock, the name of which was changed to Ayers Rock/Uluru in 1993 and reversed (in deference to Indigenous language) to Uluru/Ayers Rock in 2002. For the 1988 film, there would have been no question of using the native name, and the film also registers a crude white man's remark about the Aboriginal trackers' view of what has happened: "You can't believe those bludgers. They're always drunk." Since the events of the case and since the film, there has fortunately been some progress in matters of racial reconciliation.

In these early shots of Ayers Rock, the image of the healthy, happy, wholesome family running around on the Rock is suddenly overhung with the image of a dingo up high on the Rock, seeming to observe the happiness below. The visual juxtaposition again advances the narrative, and almost certainly at the time of the film's release it would have provoked a tremor of expectancy, the facts of the case being so widely known. The key event in the narrative arc is of course the cry in the night that announces the baby's disappearance. "A dingo's got my baby!" Lindy screams into the camp site at night.

A search party follows, police arrive, and the reactions of Lindy and Michael are recorded. In terms of motive, they have seemed the most unlikely couple to be involved, but, when no trace can be found of the baby and the Chamberlains return to their Mt. Isa home, suspicion grows and a full-scale investigation is set in place. As Roger Ebert wrote in his review: "No one else saw the tragic event take place, and the initial rush of sympathy for the parents was replaced, after a few weeks, by a malicious whispering campaign."[18] And here the core of the film's narrative and thematic importance is established: that is, the conflict that accounts for much of the film's power is that between the Chamberlains' need to assert their innocence and the vile behavior of the media and, indeed, much of the public at large. As one voice yells, "Burn the bitch!" This public often takes to crude speculation about what happened and why. As Michael says: "People can turn on you like a pack of hungry animals."

After two inquests that fail to establish guilt and with yet more investigation, including a police search of the Chamberlain's home for any possessions bearing incriminating stains of the Ayers Rock episode, the matter finally comes to court in Darwin. Here, after dealing with new evidence and further grilling of Michael, who leaves the courtroom in distress, Lindy is accused of inventing the story of the dingo as culprit. She is pronounced guilty by the jury and sentenced to imprisonment for life with hard labor, and Michael's eighteen-month sentence is suspended in the interests of his sons. By this stage, the trial has become a "show" for often-repellent spectators. Lindy, pregnant, spends several years in prison, where her baby is born, before new evidence makes clear her innocence of Azaria's death.

Returned home, she and her family, complete with the little girl to which Lindy gave birth in prison, are welcomed back into the church; there is a standing ovation from the congregation. "Praise God from Whom All Blessings Flow" swells on the soundtrack, and the film ends on a freeze-frame shot of the crowd as a voice-over intones: "How important innocence is to the innocent." In this final sequence, Schepisi has diverged from Bryson's afterword, which offered a summary of the findings that exonerated Lindy. Arguably, though, what might have been seen as a sentimentalizing can also be viewed as a kind of triumph for justice and a warning to milling crowds not to be such willing recipients of scandalous possibilities. Hence the final freeze-frame that denies the crowd a voice?

SCHEPISI'S ACHIEVEMENT

A Melbourne newspaper, recently reporting on the child-abuse conviction (now overturned) against Cardinal George Pell, invoked the Chamberlain case as an example of how "justice can go horribly pear-shaped. Lindy Chamberlain is probably the most famous example in Australia's history."[19] I quote this to suggest that thirty years later the case is still pervasively present in the collective memory and, this being so, to consider what kind of challenge it must have set Schepisi so near to the time of its progress through the courts until Lindy was finally pardoned. He had never shied clear of contentious subjects, whether matters of race, religion, and, with *A Cry in the Dark* (*Evil Angels*), legal and other issues that had preoccupied the country in sensational manner.

Adapting such material to the screen was a more demanding venture than, say, creating film versions of novels or plays, as he so often and adroitly did. He brings to the film a seriousness of purpose crucial to rendering a tragic and horrific real-life set of events. This was not just a mystery death that required to be solved; there were the lives of the actual protagonists that needed to be considered in the matter of how they would be realized on screen. As a critic wrote, on the one hand it might be seen as "a generic drama of mystery and suspense, of ambiguous motive and perhaps finally inscrutable purpose; the other is a crusading piece of cine-journalism which sets out to expose a miscarriage of justice and indict the true villains in media hysteria and public ignorance and prejudice."[20] Or as another reviewer put it: "This film is not a whodunnit. The film knows the dingo did it. This is a film about how the media did it, about how urban (and country) myth did it and how the judicial system did it to Lindy and Michael Chamberlain."[21]

Working from his and Caswell's screenplay, Schepisi handles a large cast (police, legal professionals, press and television reporters, other holiday-makers, etc.) in such a way as to allow each his or her moment, but, given the inevitably meandering nature of events over the years of investigation, he never succumbs to the conventional sense of structure that characterizes the "well-made thriller." The film has to register the prolonged anguish of the Chamberlains and the equally prolonged search for pieces of evidence.

Baker, with his cinematographic grasp of the vast and the intimate, and editor Bilcock, with her ability to put together the pieces, whether public or personal, so as to highlight their importance, whether for the moment or for the case's duration, are two of Schepisi's most pertinent collaborators in achieving its overriding tonal effect. But above all, it is Meryl Streep's incarnation of Lindy Chamberlain that is at the heart of the film's narrative and its thematic coherence. She imbues the role with a complexity that takes in the devoted wife and mother of the early episodes, the terrified discoverer of the missing child, and the sometimes strange-seeming composure that fuels some of the most disgusting public responses to her as a figure constantly in the news. In externals, her helmet of straight black hair with fringe and the simple domesticity of her clothes—tennis socks and shoes suggestive of the life she has so far lived—and the care with accent, not in any way caricatured but unobtrusively registering Lindy's New Zealand origins and decade-long Australian residence, reinforce the inner conviction she brings to the role. After registering the initial terror, Streep's Lindy is a complex *tour de force* of emotions sometimes withheld, sometimes almost violently expressed, but always subtly woven into the texture of a whole life.

Vital as Streep's participation was in getting the film made, one should not underestimate the contribution of Sam Neill's rendering of the pastor, Michael, whose reserve of manner is not at odds with the depth of the feeling that is also palpable. His religious conviction causes him to seek some element of relief in the divine purpose at work in the loss of Azaria, but there comes a time when this is not enough to sustain him through the rigors of the court proceedings, causing him to leave the courtroom abruptly when emotion overcomes him. Schepisi told an interviewer: "People will be astonished by Sam Neill, playing someone who tried to be strong and had a lot of faith and had great emotional difficulty handling the situation—it's a completely different role for him."[22] In passing, too, one recalls Schepisi's frequent preoccupation with "outsiders," and in Streep's and Neill's portrayals of the Chamberlains, the director may be said to offer a view of more or less ordinary people pushed by circumstances beyond their control, until they are as far from their usual habitat as Jimmie Blacksmith or Barbarosa.

At the time of its release, *Evil Angels/A Cry in the Dark* attracted generally good press, but there were some cavils that, thirty years on, I find harder to accept. There was ample praise for the performances of Streep and Neill, but some reservations about the way the case is presented, through the various court hearings and the renderings of public outrage.

One Australian critic felt that the film failed to "tell us *how* the media, myth and the judiciary did it"—that is, how they were responsible for the dreadful miscarriage of justice. This review goes on to suggest that "the film's perpetuation of the web of innuendo and inference spun around the disappearance [of the child] . . . inadvertently puts *Evil Angels* in the same shameful position as the much-reviled media from which it attempts to dissociate itself."[23] A British review in some respects echoes this criticism, asserting that "the film's attacks on the rumour-mongering and lurid speculation of the media—with the responses, observations and casual cynicism of various reporters and newspeople worked, patchwork-fashion, into the accounts of the trials—often seem to be pandering to the same techniques and glib judgments. In the process, the legal issues . . . raised by the two trials are none too clearly presented."[24] In the US, Roger Ebert's view more nearly approaches my own regard for what Schepisi has achieved in the matter of depicting public response (professional or otherwise). Ebert wrote: "Fred Schepisi, who directed and co-wrote the film, has used Australian public opinion as a sort of Greek chorus in the background . . . Schepisi is successful in indicting the court of public opinion, and his methodical (but absorbing) examination of the evidence helps us understand the state's circumstantial case."[25] Ebert comes closer to an understanding of how Schepisi "places" the relentless news-mongering and scandal-relishing that accompanied the affair with the phrase "indicting the court of public opinion." He also notes the way the film deals with the astounding amount of evidence that was brought to bear in the trials.

Anyone who has read Bryson's 563-page account of this will realize what a challenge Schepisi was confronting. He has not made a predictable courtroom drama from the terrible and multitudinous bits of information that had to be examined in real life, but has created a sense of the ongoing thoroughness of the investigation and of its tumultuous effect on the lives principally involved. Though "much more than a dramatized documentary . . . sadly it did not have the impact at the box office that it deserved."[26] Thirty years on, *A Cry in the Dark* stands as a highlight in Schepisi's career, pursuing demanding subject matter with critical rigor and aesthetic control.

Chapter Six

AT HOME IN THE US

With time out in Europe for *Plenty,* and Australia for the rigorous challenges of *A Cry in the Dark/Evil Angels*, Schepisi otherwise worked exclusively in US films—if not always *in* the US—for more than a decade. The films cover a genre range that includes spy thriller (*The Russia House*), romantic comedy (*Roxanne* and *I.Q.*), sports comedy-drama (*Mr. Baseball*), and an elegant version of a play that dealt in mysterious relationships (*Six Degrees of Separation*). In other words, he had shown adaptability in both working conditions and in generic choices.

THE RUSSIA HOUSE (1990)

Not Just "Another Spy Story"

Schepisi would go on to work with a number of authors notable in other media, and *The Russia House* involved him in collaboration with both novelist John le Carré, author of the antecedent novel, and playwright Tom Stoppard, who wrote the screenplay. About le Carré, Schepisi later told an interviewer: "I knew he hadn't been happy with any of the previous films based on his work. We talked for a while, and then he suggested I meet with Tom Stoppard."[1] In the event, the three "came to an agreement, forming a little pact among ourselves," and Alan Ladd Jr. at Pathé funded the writing of the first draft of *The Russia House*, which was "the first major Hollywood film to be made in the USSR that is not a co-production. It emerged as a result of a unique friendship that developed between Schepisi and director Elem Klimov, who headed the Soviet Filmmakers Union."[2]

The Russia House was Schepisi's first—indeed, only—venture into thriller territory, and it was rather daring to embark on the genre via le

Carré, whose plots are so famously intricate. Schepisi seemed to have been wary of the kinds of challenges the novel offered when he told an interviewer at the time of the film's making: "His works are very subtle, quite wordy, and there's lots of layers, all of which would seem to indicate that they are much better suited to the longer format of a television series than the normally concentrated dramatics of cinema. So it's quite a challenge to try to extract the essence of the book and present it in a very exciting way without losing the complexity and the subtlety."[3] The following account will be at least partly concerned with how—and how far—the film achieves this goal.

It is also interesting to consider in what ways it seems recognizably "a Schepisi film." Most obviously, the male protagonist, English publisher Barley Blair (Sean Connery), who lives in Lisbon, may be seen as another of those "outsider" figures who so commonly recur in his films. In terms of structure, as it darts about in time and place, *The Russia House* also recalls other Schepisi productions such as *Jimmie Blacksmith*, *Plenty*, *Evil Angels*, and, still to come, *Six Degrees of Separation*, and such procedures demand a focus that he has characteristically met by means of a protagonist whose involvement ensures viewer interest. In this case, he is on firm ground with Connery as the key figure who is brought into what proves a complex narrative web. Seven years after his last appearance as James Bond, the role that established his star persona, Connery, then aged sixty, makes of Barley a believable—and, for him, unusual—amalgam of reluctant espionage negotiator and somewhat disheveled lover. Connery himself saw Barley as "this boozy, saxophone-playing publisher, whose whole life and situation is in chaos. . . . The people he meets in Russia, and the experience of [the] moral dilemma with which he is faced, help him connect back finally to the world."[4]

The two main plot threads devolve from these aspects of the Barley character. "It is much more than just another spy story," Schepisi claimed in the interview quoted above.[5] Perhaps the idea of Connery as a literary man, a contemplative publisher who is persuaded by Ned (James Fox), a UK intelligence agent, and Russell (Roy Scheider), a CIA man from the US, to become a freelance agent to carry out investigations in Russia, helps to account for the film's avoidance of some of the expected espionage plot maneuvers. The female protagonist,

Katya (Michelle Pfeiffer), is far from the conventional lady of mystery that the genre often provided. Katya works for a Russian publisher and is asked to deliver a manuscript to Barley Blair in London. But the sales representative to whom she has passed it on at a Moscow book fair turns it over to Russian intelligence services, which stall the operations on discovering that it deals with Russia's nuclear research. The West's intelligence services prevail on Barley to return to Russia with a "shopping list" of questions to ascertain whether the author in question is really, as he suspects, "Dante" (Klaus Maria Brandauer, in a charismatic turn), a top Russian scientist whose real name is Savelev—and who is a former lover of Katya's. Finally, Barley strikes a bargain with Soviet intelligence that leads to his ensuring the safety of Katya and her children who are finally welcomed by Barney to sunny Lisbon.

The foregoing is the merest outline of the film's convoluted plot, which will be no surprise to readers of le Carré, and indeed the intricacies of narrative are both daunting and not necessarily the most compelling aspects of the film. However, one reviewer's comment about how the scenic shooting of Russian locations "severely slows down an already sluggish and impenetrable storyline" is unduly harsh.[6] Having watched the film three times in a quite short time span, my view is that the beauty of the vistas of Moscow and other Russian cities, often stunningly captured by cinematographer Ian Baker, is crucial to our understanding of Barley. He is not a usual spy but a man who actually "loves" (his word) Russia, and the vistas help to account for this. He may be wired for contact with the UK and US intelligence services, but this is not his usual territory.

Stoppard's screenplay is undoubtedly wordy, and we often have to listen to Barley's words twice, once when he says them and then when the intelligence agents hear them in their work places. These sequences, set in various offices and in a broader "glasnostic" climate, might have been strengthened by a more complex character interest in the international listeners. These latter have been smartly enough cast to have warranted more such attention. For instance, James Fox (as Ned) is consistently the reserved, polite Brit, and Roy Scheider (as Russell) is the cynical, foul-mouthed Yank, but the screenplay doesn't give them much chance to imbue their characters with other than their purely professional interest in the case—and arguably that should be enough. As Vincent Canby wrote of these and the other actors playing these roles: "[They] are all acting like actors trying very hard to find the interesting aspects of characters who have none."[7] Ken Russell, as the flamboyant Walter, is necessarily a flashy—and enjoyable—distraction, but compared with Connery and Pfeiffer, the watchers/listeners generally remain one-dimensional.

What Matters Most

This brings me to the film's real strength, which is to be found in the ways in which Barley and Katya's paths cross. What will become of Dante's manuscript and what it has to say about Soviet nuclear aspirations may set the film in motion. However, the charting of the relationship between the somewhat world-weary, aging, and beer-swigging Barley and the seemingly fragile but actually strong-minded Katya is what holds together the somewhat rambling and confusing events of the screenplay.

From the moment Barley meets up with Katya, his function as go-between for the intelligence chaps is compromised by their mutual attraction, and the two stars have rarely, if ever, been more persuasive in inhabiting their roles. Connery had by this time left far behind the Bond image: Barley could never be the sort of spy who wears a dinner suit under a diving outfit, as Connery's Bond did in the opening scene of *Diamonds Are Forever* (1971). He is not only sometimes rather shabbily dressed but he is allowed to look bit lined, with hair greying and sometimes uncombed. Costume and makeup play their parts in creating the physical Barley, but Connery, in one of his most fully achieved performances, also suggests an inner life in ways that allow us to accept Barley as a man of feeling and one with a sense of priorities. Those latter qualities are also convincingly present in Pfeiffer's Katya, who is a long way from the Bond girls. Pfeiffer's beauty has never been so gently presented, and she makes genuinely touching Katya's conflicts as one working in the interests of her country and of her family. How authentic her Russian accent is not for me to judge, but it is unerringly consistent and seems to belong utterly to what we know of Katya. The film endorses the importance of their relationship to the overall narrative by repeating, post-credits, the final episode in which Barley welcomes Katya, her children, and her uncle to Lisbon.

It seems almost to suggest that this is more important than the fate of a manuscript that two powers may be grappling over.

Roger Ebert seemed to support such a judgment when his review, expressing some weariness with the film's over-talkative espionage dealings, claimed: "What's good are the few emotional moments that break out of the weary spy formula," as when Connery declares his love for Pfeiffer.[8] As an Australian reviewer wrote: "While espionage is [the film's] master, its mistress is undoubtedly the touching parallel love story between two unlikely people."[9] In this matter, Schepisi was fortunate in having two winning performers on the order of Connery and Pfeiffer. If *The Russia House* is not Schepisi's finest hour, and if he seems less interested in charting the processes of international intelligence at work, there is real compensation in the persuasive growth of feeling between the film's protagonists. This is not to downplay the other performers in a strong cast, but these latter have less engaging material to work on. It may be also that the labyrinthine ways of le Carré are more suited to the page than to the screen.

MR. BASEBALL (1992)

This comedy of cultural clash was the "first film about Japan produced by a Japanese-owned Hollywood studio and the first test of the Japanese promise to leave creative control in Hollywood."[10] In 1991, the Matsushita Electric Industrial Co. had acquired MCA, the owner of Universal, the company that would produce the film and serve as its theatrical distributor. So, we have another example of Schepisi's coming to terms with a range of production circumstances, this time involving a need to find commercial success in Japan as well as the United States.

Schepisi Lite?

Maybe baseball enthusiasts would disagree, but some decades after its release *Mr. Baseball* feels like one of Schepisi's lesser films, and it appears to have had much more limited release than most of his films. He himself felt that it "could have been a much better film.... It was a very weird situation. The film was being done by Universal as if it was *Major League*. Then the studio was sold to Matsushita [in 1990], and the new owners wanted it changed away from *Major League* because they were fearful we were being derogatory to the Japanese."[11] There were also problems with its star, Tom Selleck, who, Schepisi hadn't realized, had script approval, and who "wanted it to be more of a baseball film than we did . . . he was nervous about his career."[12]

What emerges from this troubled start is a mildly entertaining sports comedy-drama, which moves towards somewhat obvious denouements on personal and wider social levels. For those not addicted to the game it may seem to spend too much time on the game itself and not enough in pursuing Schepisi's own views on the matter. There are five names sharing the film's writing credits: two (Theo Pelletier, John Junkerman) coauthored the story that provided the basis for the screenplay, which is the work of no fewer than three writers (Gary Ross, Kevin Wade, Monte Merrick). Perhaps a case of too many cooks stirring the broth?

That said, it can still be argued that in some respects the film offers a minor example of some of Schepisi's recurring characteristics. Yes, its protagonist is a man at odds with the space he inhabits—think of Jimmie Blacksmith, Steve Martin's C. D. Bales in *Roxanne*, let alone the titular *Iceman*. Though there is less of that mobility in time and place that characterizes some of the director's best work, such as *Six Degrees of Separation* and *Last Orders*, there is nevertheless evidence of his recurring capacity for rendering a sure sense of environment, as in *Barbarosa* or *A Cry in the Dark*. This latter trait is called into play when "Mr. Baseball" fetches up in Japan, reacting to it in ways sometimes less than tolerant. As Janet Maslin's review put it: "The real point of the film, of course, is to contrast Japanese and American modes of behavior, a comparison that seldom works in Jack's [Tom Selleck] advantage."[13] At least one reviewer would have captured Schepisi's intentions when he wrote that "the movie is as much about the culture clash between Japan and the United States as it is about baseball."[14]

A Man away from Home

The film's basic narrative impetus derives from the situation of a former Yankees baseball star, now of waning power, who relocates to Japan to join the Nagoya Dragons. He is Jack Elliot (Selleck), and, during the interview when this news is delivered to him, he replies with abrupt egoism to his agent Doc (Nicholas Gascone): "I'm a major leaguer. No way I'm going to play in Japan." Editor Peter Honess smartly cuts from this incipiently prejudiced remark to a long shot of the plane bearing Jack to Japan and subsequently to his arrival at the airport, where an interpreter translates his facetious punning comment: "I always had a yen to play here."

Jack's ego will require a few blows to blunt its edge, one of the earliest being the physical bang on the head as he fails to realize that, six-footer that he is (Selleck is actually 6'4"), his hotel accommodation has been designed for smaller people. His behavior in the country to which he has been assigned contains other such moments, some of them critical on his part (such as when, slumped in front of the TV, he switches through dozens of channels without finding anything to his liking). His ego is further punctured when a woman at the baseball center suggests dinner at 9 o'clock. In such matters, Jack has been used to calling the shots.

More crucially from a professional perspective, he refuses to join in the Dragons' training ritual, instead putting the team through a series of idiotic exercises of *his* devising. As a further example of his disrespect, sometimes enacted for comedy, sometimes for more serious reproach, he spits on the Dragons' field, which is "considered sacred." After training, he flops into a bath whereas the rest of the team must wash before bathing: that is, he is out of step with the Japanese way—and doesn't care. "Do I need someone to teach me how to take a crap?" he asks, being quite sure of what the answer should be. And with equal certainty that he knows best, he announces, "I'll deal with the press," dismissing more respectful reporting.

Unsurprisingly, the film moves towards Jack's gradual acquiring of respect for the Japanese culture and towards his burgeoning romance with Hiroko (Ava Takanashi), the advertising professional who had taken the initiative about their first dinner date. These two elements in the plot find some useful narrative integration. When Ava takes him to visit her grandparents, there is a neat comic episode as he tries unsuccessfully to deal with chopsticks—and with sitting at table on the floor—pointing to his incapacity to adjust to cultural differences. "Grow up!" Hiroko shouts at him, and from this starting point, Jack will make a more serious attempt to deal with the team. At the grandparents' home, he has also discovered that Ava is the daughter of his manager (Ken Takakura), with whom he has been on fractious terms.

This movement to greater tolerance on Jack's part and to his ensuing success on the baseball field is a largely predictable regeneration, as are his relationship with Ava and his conciliatory hug with her unsmiling father. Though Schepisi wanted *Mr. Baseball* to be less of "a baseball film," and though the baseball sequences can seem wearisome, it needs to be accepted that the film does take the game seriously, as if there were more to it than merely how it re-lights Jack's fading star. The stadium shots have a convincing authenticity. Also, as Roger Ebert aptly wrote of Ava's function: "There is, of course, a woman . . . and for once she is not a clone of the stereotyped quasi-geisha; she's an advertising professional who runs the club's enforcements."[15] Indeed, this avoidance of cliché strengthens the film's somewhat straggling narrative practices.

Maybe a subtler actor than Selleck, whose hirsute torso gets more sightings than are good for him or the film, might have resulted in a tougher-minded movie. As it is, the touches of comedy are too fleeting and the representation of cultural clash too facile in its resolution. In this matter, the *Washington Post* review may be too severe in dismissing the film as "a weak attempt to promote a feeling of hands-across-the-water congeniality between the two countries" and is certainly so in describing the humor as "condescending."[16] *Mr. Baseball* has its diverting moments, but on the whole it lacks the coherence Schepisi has characteristically brought to bear on multi-textured experiences.

SIX DEGREES OF SEPARATION (1993)

The idea that everyone is separated from everyone else by no more than six degrees has no doubt proliferated with John Guare's play of that name and the Schepisi film adaptation, but its actual origin goes back to 1929, when Hungarian writer Frigyes Karinthy proposed it in a short story titled *Chains*. The play and the film, in their different modes, make dazzling use of the concept. Both, in turn, were based on actual events involving "a young 19-year-old black by the name of David Hampton [who] gained notoriety in 1983 . . . by passing himself off as David Poitier, the reputed son of Sidney Poitier," who betrayed the hospitality of a couple who took him in for the night, was subsequently arrested on criminal charges, sentenced to four years in prison, and died of AIDS-related causes in 2003.[17] John Guare based his play on what he heard and read of this story, and "except for the conclusion, the film's plot follows that of the earlier stage production," changing the names of the real-life people involved.[18]

Another Kind of Adaptation

Schepisi had the experience of working on adaptations of other media to film, but filming Guare's *Six Degrees of Separation* presented a very different set of challenges—and Schepisi seems genuinely to have welcomed such challenges. He sought to do justice to the preceding work while making something new of it, "interpreting the work in your own way," as he said:

> It was the same with *Six Degrees*, a play, and there were people who wouldn't make it because they've seen the play which was presented in a very surrealistic way with people coming out of the audience to tell their story, then going back into the audience while the boy was up there on the stage. I had no intention of doing it when I went to see it as a play. I went to see it again with two of my older children and there were elements of the play that related to them, so I saw something else in it.[19]

When he met Guare, who would eventually write the screenplay, the playwright had already seen several of Schepisi's films and been impressed with how he had dealt with the ways in which his protagonists had responded to their settings and cultures. For instance, he admired the use of the setting in *Roxanne*, "not as just a picture postcard, but [in the way] that town exerted a force on all the magical things that happened in that movie, and [in filming *Six Degrees*] I wanted New York to have the same feeling."[20] Schepisi also wanted to make "a real New York movie," so that he and Guare appear to have been of like mind when they met. As author Gordon E. Slethaug wrote in a detailed and perceptive account: "This combined panorama of the city and depiction of wealth and comfort at the beginning of the film supplements, exceeds, and displaces that of the drama in its realism, texture and sense of place."[21]

Guare also recalled Schepisi's saying that "he loved the way the play was structured ... and he wanted to find the cinematic equivalent of it."[22] There had been considerable interest in the prospect of filming the play, but when Guare and Schepisi met up the deal was made and Guare was taken with how the cinema's fluidity might go to work on his play—and presumably how he as screenwriter might lay the basis for this adaptation.

The resulting film is one of Schepisi's most complex and most adventurous works, in terms of ideology, genre, and technique, while still retaining elements identified in the earlier stages of his filmography. The "outsider," perhaps the most frequently recurring protagonist in his films, is again at the heart of *Six Degrees*, his presence leading to matters of cultural collision and problems of communication. In genre terms, it is one of the most difficult of his films to categorize, exhibiting, in its elegant hybridity, elements of comedy of manners, family drama, and social document. In terms of technique, its deployment of a prowling camera and often through incessant talk exhibits an utterly fluid dealing with time and place. Guare's play is revealed through ninety minutes of nonstop talk, with no interval. In the play's text, characters' lines are sometimes followed by the words "(*To us*)," which means that such lines are delivered directly to the audience.[23] Another challenge to the filmmaker is in the occasions when a character talks uninterrupted for pages at a time.[24] In its utterly different way, *Six Degrees* must have made demands on Schepisi as rigorous as those he dealt with when making *A Cry in the Dark*.

From Complex Play to Complex Film

We expect that plays will engage in continuous talk, but it is not often that this is expected—or even welcomed—in the cinematic mode of audio-visual moving images. However, Schepisi has found a set of procedures that will enable this. He recalled: "Almost everybody doubted that you could make it work on film, because it was so locked into theatre conventions.... There was a time when I thought I might have the characters telling their story directly to camera, but then I rejected that. My approach was to put the camera in among them, like you were sitting at the table or that party or event with them."[25] Whereas the talk on stage will naturally be confined to one audience on every occasion, in Guare's screenplay the characters are placed in a range of settings, meaning that the audience keeps changing.

Ouisa Kittredge (Stockard Channing) and her art-dealer husband Flan (Donald Sutherland), still in evening attire, are first seen frantically moving about their elegant New York apartment and talking of the wedding they are running late to attend. The film cuts to a young Black guy, Paul (Will Smith), addressing someone (or no one?) in a modest room adorned with a bicycle. When the Kittredges arrive at the wedding, they start talking to other guests about "last night" and, in the ensuing episodes, the film glides between "today" and "last night" as other guests—and eventually even the bridal couple—gather around Ouisa and Flan.

In this way, the core plot (though the word sounds almost too conventional) is set in motion as they describe how their intended dinner with a rich friend from South Africa, Geoffrey (Ian McKellen), is interrupted by the arrival of Paul, who claims to be a university friend of the Kittredges' children, and who says he has been mugged and stabbed in Central Park. This is not just a matter of (mainly) Ouisa talking to the wedding guests: the film, abetted by Peter Honess's editing, flashes back and forth between her talking and her activities as hostess during the previous night, while her audience at the wedding grows. The wedding guests are the cinematic equivalents of the theatre audience to whom Guare's characters often addressed remarks.

Paul arrived at the Kittredges' Fifth Avenue apartment when they were entertaining Geoffrey, the gold magnate whose financial backing Flan needs to effect the sale of a Cézanne to Japanese investors. Whatever the facts of Paul's story—and they are almost nonexistent—the lifestyle of the Kittredges also comes in for some sophisticated evaluation. Matters of art, and its financial potential, are crucial to their privileged existence, which Paul's arrival will threaten. In the film's last episode, Ouisa walks out of a fashionable dinner party at which she has been telling how (and the film cuts to where and when) she has tried to help Paul, who has been taken away by police. News has subsequently been heard of a young Black man who has hanged himself in jail. She is not sure this news refers to Paul, and, when she and Flan try to explain why they were "taken in" by him, someone asks: "Why does it mean so much to you?" Ouisa insists: "It was an experience. I will not turn him into an anecdote." At odds with the stylish diners, she leaves abruptly, followed by an embarrassed Flan, whereas in the play, though she may have arrived at a more thoughtful approach to the events, she does not leave.

At this point, rupture between them occurs. Flan berates her because their hostess, Mrs. Bannister (Kitty Carlisle Hart), is important to his art-dealer business, and Ouisa turns on him, saying, "You are a terrible man," and walks away alone. Paul, whose image she imagines she sees in a florist's window, has penetrated her imaginative life, leading her to realize that there may be more to living than the hitherto lavishly upholstered circumstances she has known.

Between the wedding sequence and the dinner party, two of the main occasions when the film deals with the play's mode of audience address, other characters whose worlds Paul has infiltrated emerge and contribute their experiences to the richly stimulating texture of the film. Another couple who are friends of the Kittredges, Kitty and Larkin (Mary Beth Hurt and Bruce Davison), recount what they believe to be a unique experience with Paul, only to find the Kittredges have had the same, and a doctor (Richard Masur) has given him a key to his house. The children of all three houses invaded by Paul—or did they simply let him into their lives?—are outraged by what they perceive to be their parents' gullible behavior.

Reviewing the film at the time of its release, I wrote: "What emerges as the narrative twists and turns is a stripping away of layers of complacency and self-absorption, as the catalytic figure of Paul cuts a swathe through one group after another."[26] Several viewings later, that still seems an apt statement of the underlying idea that welds this structurally complex film together. All three of the houses that have admitted Paul—and the offspring of those parents—will be forced to come to terms with not just this experience but also how it reflects on the wider pattern of their lives, though it is only Ouisa who is seen to be significantly changed by it.

This is not to suggest that the film descends into schematism, but that its holding power is in the various ways in which Paul's intrusion is received in different, if connected, circumstances. For instance, the responses of the young people to how their parents have reacted are as much a matter of varied intra-familial tensions, these sharpened by this stranger/con man. There is also another young man, Trent Conway (Anthony Michael Hall), and his girlfriend, whom Paul meets in Central Park, where he spins a tale about being Flan's illegitimate son, as fictitious as his earlier claim of being Sidney Poitier's son. Trent trains Paul in how to be "the most sought-after young man in the east"; in other words, his training has been responsible for enabling Paul to present himself so plausibly. In return for his efforts, Paul seduces Trent and steals their savings, leading Trent to commit suicide.

Paul's racial situation may elicit some sympathy for him, but it is not allowed to absolve him of his con-man deceptions. He may draw attention to the ever-widening gap between the privileged classes, the "haves," and the "have-nots" in his society, but *Six Degrees* is not to be categorized as some sort of morality play. Schepisi keeps the film moving from a range of luxurious settings to contrasting insertions of less affluent locations, but the superb vistas of the New York skyline, brilliantly caught by Ian Baker's camera, have the curious effect of eliding these contrasts, as if to suggest that there may be more at stake than physical and social disparity. What goes on in the imagination or the heart may not be constrained by the externally visible.

Six Degrees may well be Schepisi's most riveting US film. He has shown himself adaptable to popular genres in such diverse pieces as *Barbarosa* and *Roxanne*, but arguably none has made such stylistic demands in the unfolding of a complex scenario as does his bringing of Guare's idiosyncratic piece to film life. The above reference to Ian Baker leads one to consider how impressively well served Schepisi has been by his collaborators in this venture. Of course, Guare's own adaptation of his play into another medium is the starting point.

It was Guare also who urged the casting of Stockard Channing as Ouisa, recreating the role she had played so successfully on stage.

Channing may have "described doing *Six Degrees* on film as like putting the toothpaste back in the tube," as Schepisi recalled,[27] but it is perhaps above all her performance that most securely anchors the film. It is she who allows that "an experience," such as that offered by Paul's intrusion, may profoundly affect the life you have been taking for granted. And Will Smith imbues Paul with the sort of charm and effortless duplicity that helps account for the initial responses from those whose lives he invades, as well as with something further that ensures and accounts for Ouisa's life's taking a different turn. Maybe this involves an education of the imagination, suggesting perhaps that the Kittredges' world of privilege does not answer all the needs of living.

Among the others responsible for the film's overall sheen, Patrizia von Brandenstein's production design is important in establishing from the outset the elegant affluence of the Kittredges' lifestyle. The spacious apartment with its glowing red walls and handsome furnishings and other artifacts, including gilt-framed paintings and mirrors, and the New York skyline seen from its wide windows, is a triumph of design, and this is all caught immaculately by Baker's prowling camera. This was Baker's tenth partnership with the director, so presumably by now he knew what Schepisi had in mind. Further, as the camera moves from wide shots of the apartment or other settings such as art galleries, New York's cavernous streets, or Mrs. Bannister's stately dining room, to close-ups of individuals talking, or between the pivotal night and the occasions when it is recalled, design and camera are adroitly served by Peter Honess's discreet editing. And to name one more collaborator, composer Jerry Goldsmith underlays the film's visual patina with a score that draws with an irresistible eclecticism that embraces everyone from Wagner to Cole Porter and thereby adds another dimension of meaning.

According to another editor, Jill Bilcock, who worked with Schepisi on *A Cry in the Dark* and *I.Q.*, the director had ways of uniting and drawing out the best from cast and crew. She recalled him as

> an extraordinary presence on set, full of enthusiasm and love of life. He's highly energetic on the set, and that enthuses people around him and makes them step up a bit. He's very involved

in the whole process, he makes people feel at ease about contributing to his work. And from an artistic point of view? He's a good storyteller; not so strong on music. Jerry Goldsmith was a very profound composer. Fred just loves people around him and he likes being a leader. He's not indecisive about creative matters. He'd be involved in discussion with Ian Baker about how he wanted a scene to look.[28]

Six Degrees is one of the most telling examples, among many, of Schepisi's capacity to unite the contributions of before- and behind-camera personnel in the service of a complex amalgam of sight and sound. A quarter-century later, it seems a strikingly modern piece of work that makes stimulating use of the cinema's resources. It was generally well received, with the odd cavil: one US reviewer labeled it "less a drama than an exercise in cuteness,"[29] and a UK critic, while finding it "a wonderful piece of story-telling," ended his review by declaring that "the film is a dazzling but determinedly superficial affair."[30] My final response would be that, yes, it is "dazzling," but that one of its strengths lies in its *critique* of superficiality, of how lives lived thus can fail to take on board more serious matters—such as, for instance, the power of the imagination to extend those lives.

I.Q. (1994)

Set in New Jersey in the Eisenhower era (and the president turns up briefly as a character in the plot), *I.Q.* has a nice, understated sense of period, which, more than twenty-five years later, continues to contribute to the film's charm. It seems to have been filmed entirely on various locations in New Jersey, including Princeton, the setting for some of its key comic moments, and elsewhere there is a pleasing aura of lived-in streets and houses, cafés, bars—and, crucial in plot terms, a garage, the latter (and renovated) in nearby Hopewell, New Jersey.

The film's central narrative mover is that of depicting Albert Einstein (Walter Matthau) as a matchmaker. The scientific genius spent the last twenty-two years of his life in the US, pursuing his career at Princeton University, while the film has him sharing what prove to be his last days with three other clever old scientists (Kurt Godel [Lou Jacobi], Boris Podolsky [Gene Katz], and Nathan Liebknecht [Joseph Mayer]), and his niece, Catherine (Meg Ryan). Schepisi said at the time: "I liked . . . the whimsy of the fact that Einstein, who lived in his own head for much of his life, is suddenly trying to calculate how to put two people together. I liked the notion that Einstein doesn't want his niece, who is also living in her head, to make the same mistakes in life that he did."[31] Catherine also happens to be a genius and wants to marry a comparably gifted chap. To this end, she has become engaged to a rather pompous scholar (a not unusual type in American comedy) called James Moreland (Stephen Fry), a psychology professor. As such, James may be supposed to understand human nature but not much about cars, and when he and Catherine are driving his unsuitably small red car it develops a problem, leading them to seek help at a garage. Here, one of the three mechanics is the amiable Ed Walters (Tim Robbins), who obviously knows a lot about cars but is also surprisingly acute about the workings of the heart, and he grasps at once that he and Catherine are made for each other. "It was like death but in a good way," he sums it up, as a vision of the future—and the basis for the film's romantic plot. About the latter, several commentators compared the way the film brings together two such unlike people with the screwball comedies of much earlier decades: J. Hoberman in the *Village Voice* summed it up as "this variation on a venerable screwball theme (see *Ball of Fire*, 1941),"[32] and the reviewer for the *West Australian* also saw "the sweetly eccentric professors as direct descendants of the European geniuses in the 1941 screwball classic *Ball of Fire*."[33]

The meeting of the young couple is set up in the first quarter-hour, with images of the old guys out walking, Catherine and James in a restaurant talking about color choices, and Ed getting on with his work at the garage when Catherine enters and his everyday life takes on a new dimension. These introductory moments are accompanied by Jerry Goldsmith's absurdly engaging score with its variations on "Twinkle, Twinkle, Little Star."

The contrast between twittish Pom and husky American, what accounts for Catherine's interest in either, and then Albert and his mates' discussion of how "everything happens by chance"—these elements are all in place when Ed, having found Catherine's watch left in the garage, calls at Einstein's home to return it. At this point, the rest of the plot is set in motion, when Ed engages the support of Einstein and "the three greatest minds of the twentieth century . . . who can't change a light bulb." The likable mechanic, who is no genius but "a fan" of Einstein, rescues some of the old guys' objects that have been lost in a tree, from which Ed then falls, establishing the dangers of gravity as well as securing the backing of the elderly quartet, who shortly after are seen benignly discerning "an unmistakable chemical reaction" as they watch Ed and Catherine walk away.

This more than usually detailed account of the film's opening episodes is intended to establish the fact that Schepisi is working from a screenplay (coauthored by Andy Breckman and Michael Leeson, from Breckman's story) that will continue, abetted again by Jill Bilcock's deft editing, to weave all its threads together with charm and wit. As romantic comedies go, it is both genuinely romantic and often very funny in its inventiveness.

So How Does It Work Out?

Einstein and his old buddies now decide to set Ed up as a genius and to promote the idea of Catherine's going out with him. Some of the film's best comedy derives from the former enterprise with Ed being presented as guest lecturer at a Princeton symposium at which he is to deliver a paper on nuclear fusion. The old guys' aim is for him to impress Catherine with his hidden abilities, and Ed is, of course, very apprehensive about this, but the scientists send him cues from the audience, and there are some very funny moments as Ed, inspired by Catherine's presence, reacts to acclaim. It's as though the film wants to portray the scientist as something more than a stuffy old ivory tower-dweller, and this notion is clinched when Einstein fakes a heart attack to prevent the pompous James from intervening between Ed and Catherine.

It is a quite daring move to bring Einstein into the plot of a "romcom," but Walter Matthau's performance as the émigré genius is one of *I,Q.*'s major strengths. He resists making the scientist merely a cuddly old dear doing his best for his niece: he recognizes her intellectual gifts and acknowledges her academic aspirations but wants her to be aware of the demands of the heart as well. As for Ed, the old man sees in him a sweet-natured guy who can admire Catherine's achievements but who loves her for herself, and the film allows Ed a touching self-knowledge that leads him to explain the reward of being "taken seriously by some pretty extraordinary people." Ed knows he's allowed himself to be a fraud in the symposium hall, but he does have a real interest in science-related matters. "We squeezed the brains a little to make room for the heart," says Einstein to the old guys in one of the later shots of the quartet watching as the young couple walk off together.

Most critics admired Matthau's incarnation of Einstein, and Matthau himself claimed that "he benefitted from the unsolicited expertise of Princeton locals who had actually known or seen Einstein"[34]. Roger Ebert labeled him "a stroke of casting genius. He looks uncannily like the great mathematician,"[35] while another, much later, writer praised him thus: "The biggest surprise is what Schepisi manages to do with Matthau . . . [he] managed to get Matthau to play it slow, play it cool, and play with a charming grin on the face . . . it completely works. Matthau makes Einstein a completely human character, one that has a lighter side as well as a serious side."[36] And the *Washington Post* reviewer enthused that "Einstein . . . is hilariously brought to life by Walter Matthau."[37] One of the few less positive reviews criticized Einstein's buddies as "each progressively more of a caricature of the Jewish Eastern European émigré than Matthau's Einstein, who is played as an unkempt, caring uncle with a talent for self-deprecating one-liners."[38]

This last comment, in my view, undervalues the warmth of feeling that Matthau and the others bring to their function in setting up Ed with an equation that makes him appear an expert on space travel and nuclear fusion. They do so, partly because they find him an amiable contrast to the chilly, petulant James, and mainly because they want Catherine to realize that there is more to life than academic success, that heart matters at least as much as brain. In Robbins and Ryan, Schepisi has performers of a believable charm and naturalness. Perhaps the film might have allowed the James character a little more scope to reveal what has drawn him to Catherine, but arguably, in

Ryan and Robbins, Schepisi established the most appealing romantic pairing of his career. As Janet Maslin wrote: "[Though] *I.Q.* has become a little silly in terms of plot . . . the main characters are so strong that the film's gentle pleasures persist even when its focus drifts."[39] And Hal Hinson, describing the film as "disarming piffle—frothy, sweet and nearly irresistible," agreed that "the real attraction here is in the rapport between these two enormously appealing stars."[40] In Australia, Barbara Creed found it "a charming, zany comedy with just the right touch of whimsy. It shrewdly suggests that the little things of life, like love and romance, may well be governed by the same mathematical laws that look after the universe."[41] On the whole, the film was well received, and there was regular praise for the acting of Ryan, Robbins, and Matthau, even as there were some reservations about the plotting. One such reviewer felt that these performances "manage to keep *I.Q.* on the road for the first hour or so, [but] the poorly constructed screenplay causes the wheels to fall off in the bumpy run home."[42] This is not a view I share but is quoted simply to indicate that it wasn't all smooth sailing critically for the film.

Schepisi had had problems with getting the screenplay together, with writers being "shunted out" and replaced,[43] though, on viewing twenty-five years later, it maintains an overall tone utterly suited to its romantic comedy genre. *I.Q.* may not be Schepisi's most challenging project, but it is executed with wit, precision, and a touch of genuine feeling. As to the latter quality, one is reminded of his success in establishing the romantic rapport between Connery and Pfeiffer in *The Russia House*.

FIERCE CREATURES (1997)

"I just came into that to help fix it up," was Schepisi's comment when I mentioned this film to him.[44] And this notion was borne out by several other similar dismissals of the film. For example, in another interview he gave as reasons for getting involved with a "film [that] had been finished, and . . . was a mess": "It was a comedy, John Cleese was involved, I needed some money, and I asked for and received a reasonable amount of it. And I did it as a favor."[45] In spite of these motives, it became the film "to which he wishes he'd never attached his name."[46] And, in a critical article on Schepisi's films much later, Dan Callahan wrote: "Schepisi has sometimes been at the mercy of his material; he could do nothing to salvage the misbegotten comedy, *Fierce Creatures*."[47]

Of course, what exactly the situation was that Schepisi inherited is difficult—perhaps impossible—to determine. The film's credits read "Directed by Robert Young & Fred Schepisi," the non-alphabetic order presumably indicating the respective degrees—if not necessarily significance—of the contribution of each to the finished product. The British journal *Sight & Sound* tactfully says that, after "negative test screenings in the US . . . Schepisi shot the new ending because Young was 'unavailable.'"[48] Young had had plenty of experience as director and producer across a range of genres, perhaps best known for the black comedy, *Splitting Heirs* (1993), and the TV series *G.B.H.* (1991), and these had involved him with the likes of John Cleese, Michael Palin, Eric Idle, and others who would make their presences felt in *Fierce Creatures*. He seems not, on the basis of various comments, to have been ideally suited to the comic, satirical, even farcical demands of the film.

Hovering over the film—an intertextual element of no help to its reception or reputation—was the hugely successful, award-winning comedy, *A Fish Called Wanda* (1988), directed by Charles Crichton, the Ealing Studios veteran of such classics as *The Lavender Hill Mob* (1951). Actually, *Wanda* was co-directed by John Cleese (uncredited), who also wrote its screenplay, and would coauthor that for *Fierce Creatures*. To confirm the lineage, the earlier film starred Cleese, Palin, Jamie Lee Curtis, and Kevin Kline, who were again the starring quartet in *Fierce Creatures*. There would be some of the same touches of black comedy, in relation to animals for instance, and some anti-American echoes (which had never harmed the US box-office success of *Wanda*), but, despite some of the same ingredients of theme, comedy, and personnel, *Fierce Creatures* never stood a chance.

Chapter Seven

TRIUMPH IN THE UK— *LAST ORDERS* (2002)

In what may well be his finest achievement, the British-made *Last Orders*, some of Schepisi's recurring characteristics receive their most eloquent outings. If there is not an "outsider" protagonist in the more literal sense of, say, *Barbarosa* or *Six Degrees of Separation*, it could be said that Jack Dodds, whose "last orders" the film pursues, is at a remove from the other key figures because he's dead, and his "presence" in the film will depend on how he is recollected. Further, the fluidity of movement in time and place—and, in this case, memory—is among the ongoing strengths of Schepisi's work. And, third, his experience as an adapter of works in other media is here tested as rigorously as it was in *Six Degrees*, and with comparable astuteness.

Whenever British cinema seems to take an upward turn, it is almost invariably because of a new burst of realism. This was the case in such key periods of its history as the wartime and postwar cinema of the 1940s and the "New Wave" successes of the late '50s/early '60s. Now, at the time of Schepisi's making *Last Orders* in England, there had been a new upsurge of quality realist productions from the likes of Ken Loach, Mike Leigh, and Michael Winterbottom. As in the best of realist filmmaking, it's not just a matter here of pointing the camera at "ordinary lives." There may be nothing remarkable in the lives of the main characters in *Last Orders*, but in evoking the way they live, what they have in common and what distinguishes them from each other, director-screenwriter Schepisi always manages to suggest that larger issues—such as the lingering aftereffects of world war—are at stake. He achieves this not by spelling out such significance but by his very precise attention to the details of the lives of five men and one woman. There is a powerful whiff of reality about it all and we end by suspecting that there are no such things as "ordinary lives": all lives are particular, special in their own ways. Reality is not the same as realism, but realism, in relation to time and place for instance, is one of the ways by which we can be confronted with reality. So are, say, comedy or melodrama, but realism has most often been the British way.

FILMMAKER AND AUTHOR

Graham Swift

Swift's *Last Orders*[1] was the Booker Prize–winning novel of 1996 and must have presented some serious challenges to the filmmaker adapting it to the screen. It is structured around a journey to sprinkle the ashes of a dead friend, Jack Dodds, from Margate Pier. The journey is interspersed with the memories of those making it; and there are frequent changes in first-person narrators, whether in the present or in the past. There are seventy "sections": "chapters" seems perhaps too conventional a word to conjure up what is being brought to the surfaces in these. They vary wildly in length from a couple of sentences on a single page to more than a half-dozen pages. Some recollections take longer than others; some are more intricate than others, telling us more about what is recalled and who is doing the recalling.

Most sections are headed with the name of the person whose memories are being evoked. However, there are also several headings that refer to key stopping-places along the way. The first is Bermondsey, where, in a pub, a different kind of "last orders" is being indulged before the chaps get started on the journey to carry out those other last orders of their old friend; and there are other sections bearing the names of places such as Chatham, Wick's Farm, and Canterbury, all of which are significant markers on the way to Margate, which is the final title.

Schepisi and Swift

As quoted earlier, Schepisi summed up his attitude to adaptation as "playing around" with the antecedent text but as "doing justice to the original work, not just us[ing] it as a springboard" for your own work."[2]

So, how then does he deal with the seventy-section structure of the novel to create a comparable sense of the carrying out of the last orders and of what surfaces in the minds of the four men along the way? He recalled his dealings with Swift as being entirely amicable and in the interests of producing the film he had in mind. He explained this as follows:

> In *Last Orders*, in the novel, one chapter's done from this person's point of view, and the next from another's, and so on. I refer to that as the surface point of the novel, which was written that way for a reason. My task then is to find a movie way of presenting that and when I have done that I'm delivering in film terms the spirit of what's in the novel. I kept Graham Swift involved, he'd give me fifteen pages of notes, I'd say this or that doesn't work on film, and we had a great relationship. He'd had a bit of a block for a while, but when we started to do the film he got unblocked and started writing again. He used to write in the morning, then he'd come and visit us on the set in the afternoon. The last day of the film was difficult. We shot it in Margate, everything was worked out, but I said: "Where's Swifty gone?" Someone said, "He's over there behind that bunker . . . he's crying." I went over to him and said: "Did it get to you?" and he said: "I can't tell you how exactly it is as I'd imagined it!"[3]

Swift is not formally credited as contributing to the film's screenplay, but it is clear from Schepisi's recollections that his input was valued by the director—and that the author valued the director's interpretation of his novel.

Given Schepisi's views on adaptation and what is owed to the antecedent text, it will be important to consider how he deals with its narrative flexibility. The novel may be structured around the journey and its purpose, but it also evokes a tangle of lives, which over fifty years have interacted with each other, sometimes happily, sometimes not, and which are now the matter of diverse memories. Just as "chapters" seemed too formal for the novel's sections, so, in the film, "flashbacks" will often sound unduly disruptive of the forward narrative flow, whereas "memory sequences" gives a more accurate sense of their frequently fleeting nature, sometimes no more than a couple of moments set in motion by a word from one of the men in the car. His cinematographer, Brian Tufano, responded to the demands of this kind of visual fluidity, recalling with satisfaction his collaboration with the director: "The great thing about Fred was that he has imagination and he knows exactly what he wants, and the challenge for me was to find ways to help him achieve exactly that."[4] As will become clear in examination of specific episodes, the meeting of these challenges is crucial to the film's narrative texture.

A flashback in film is a more finite sequence for a special purpose, perhaps triggered by a specific act of storytelling by a character, but I think there is something closer to poetry in Schepisi's use of brief memory inserts. They illuminate the character doing the remembering as much as those others who are being recollected.

Not many films adapted from novels keep as closely to the contours of the original as does *Last Orders*. The only film in recent years that matches it for this kind of adherence is the adaptation of Julian Barnes's novel, *The Sense of an Ending*. Reviewing the latter at the time, I wrote: "When I re-read the book just before seeing the film, I was reminded how idiosyncratic it is. Watching it on the screen, directed by Ritesh Batra from a screenplay by Nick Payne, gave me the strangest feeling of watching the *translation* of a narrative in one medium into another that just happened to be using a language system consisting of audio-visual moving images."[5] On occasion in *Last Orders* (as in Batra's film), this comes near to transliteration, and yet there is nothing merely slavish about this. Rather, in Schepisi's own words quoted above, he has sought to do justice to the novel while, at the same time, rendering its concerns in filmic terms.

FOUR ON THE ROAD—AND OTHERS

As in Swift's novel, the film opens in a pub called the Coach and Horses (the name already suggests a trip!), where four men gather for a drink. These are Ray Johnson (Bob Hoskins), a divorced and retired insurance salesman in his sixties, with a reputation for lucky racetrack betting; Lenny Tate (David Hemmings), ex-boxer who runs a fruit-and-vegetable stall; undertaker Vic Tucker (Tom Courtenay); and, the last to arrive, the much-younger Vince Dodds (Ray Winstone), who runs his own secondhand car salesroom. Vince arrives, in his plushy Mercedes (or "Merc" as it is called), with a box containing the ashes of the old friend of the senior three and "father" of Vince. It was the last wish of butcher Jack Dodds (Michael Caine) that his remains should be scattered to the winds off Margate pier, to which he had always hankered to return. They are all used to meeting in this pub and Vic explains to their friendly barman Bernie (George Innes) the purpose of the trip they are about to make from the Bermondsey site of the Coach and Horses to Margate.

The shape of the film, as indicated above, is dictated by this journey in the Mercedes that Vince has brought for the occasion. But in spite of this narrative structure, *Last Orders* is not really a "road movie" in the usual sense of the term. Certainly, we take in the changing settings along the way, and there are several important stops, but what essentially "happens" along the way are the recollections of the four in the form of memory sequences. There isn't a lot of action in the film's present, except on the occasion of a punch-up between Vince and the querulous Lenny in a muddy hopfield. The real drama is in the way bits of the various, sometimes interlocking pasts of the four filter out of their rambling conversations. As one writer observed, the film "relies for its cumulative power on flashbacks triggered by chance words or gestures—a comment on the handwriting on the dead man's will, for instance, sparks off a shot of him scrawling on a blackboard."[6] I may quibble over the use of the term "flashback," but the writer makes exactly the point about how the film is working.

It would be tedious to go through the whole film to explore how in its audio-visual images it captures the novel's moving about in time and place. However, it is worth exploring, through a couple of passages of the film, the ways in which Schepisi's treatment of the narrative impulses that propel Swift's novel reflect the director's views on adaptation, without ever seeming to espouse a merely dogged fidelity to the antecedent text.

The opening episode referred to above sets the film's tone in establishing the four men who will undertake to carry out the last orders in virtually the same sequence as that of the novel. And, as in the novel, there is a brief memory flash to the last time they were all in the pub with Jack, on the occasion of Vince's fortieth birthday.

Back in the film's present, there is talk of Jack's widow, Amy (Helen Mirren), who is not joining them, because "she'll be seeing June, as per usual." The film then cuts to another present to reveal Amy in a red coat boarding a red London bus to visit Jack's and her mentally disabled daughter in "a home," as she has been doing regularly for fifty years, on what Jack has called "a fool's errand" because June has never shown a flicker of recognition of Amy's presence.

All this is established within the first twelve minutes of the film (and in the first three "sections" or "chapters" of the novel), in brief snatches of talk and images of past and present (in the pub), and here and there (the pub and the bus). Schepisi's dexterity in storytelling is brilliantly articulated here—as it will be throughout the film—by Peter Honess's editing and Tufano's cinematography. The fact that Amy is wearing a red coat identical in color to the bus she always boards on her way to see June seems in its small way utterly to align her with the purpose symbolized by the bus. On the day of the Margate venture, Amy speaks to June, but elicits no more than the usual response— "They must be there by now"—and goes on to carry out her own "last orders" to herself by adding, "I've got to think of me own future." This is her final goodbye to June, who, of course, won't register any change. Amy, both on the bus and with her sense of what her future must now be, is, in her way, as much "on the road" as the men now are, approaching New Cross in South London.

As one commentator at the time wrote, after averting to some of the difficulties of the film's production ("lousy British weather, allotted money that didn't come through, a tight schedule"), "the result traces the complicated shared history of four East Londoners"[7] among whom relations have not always been easy. As, in some cases, they have not been in their dealings with the late Jack, who proves to be the key figure, but as Schepisi said, "[it] isn't about individuals; it's about the group and how necessary the people in the group are to one another. It's the currents that are flowing between them at all times."[8]

The recollections and reminiscences of the chaps in the Merc are still at the heart of the film's meaning as they are in the novel. These are still what *happens* on the trip, but Schepisi takes full advantage of the cinema's effortless mobility in time and place. Whereas the novel devotes a "chapter" to the memory flight of this or that man, the film can cut from the car's interior to, say, Jack's butcher's shop on the day he told Ray he's planning to sell up, or for a fleeting moment while Vince and wife Mandy (Sally Hurst) comfort Amy when she has just learned that Jack's illness is terminal. If this cinematic mobility has any real comparison with literature, it is not so apparent in a novel—even one as flexible as Swift's—as in poetry where a word may evoke another time or place in a passing reference.

The film retains the novel's reliance on such recollection and, without ever causing confusion, is not afraid to transport us from the present confinement in the Merc to the moment in the past—and *then* from that moment to another still further back in another past. Schepisi's technique is so sure that we are never in doubt about whose past we are inhabiting at any given moment. Again, too, Tufano's camera prowls the inside of the Merc as effortlessly as it does the streets and landscape through which it is travelling.

THREE STOPOVERS

Place, whether in past or present, whether inside the Merc or in Jack's hospital ward or in June's "home," is always crucial to how we receive the information about character and relationships. Three stopovers of major significance during the journey from the Bermondsey pub in East London to Margate Pier, where the "last orders" will be executed, are made as the Merc makes its way across the Kentish countryside. In their own ways, each stopover has its bearing on the film and novel's very resonant title.

Chatham

When they are finishing their lunch, Vic, who has been in the navy during the war, suggests they make a small detour to visit the Chatham Naval War Memorial. There's been talk over lunch about Jack and Ray's army experiences, and brief flashes to when, as young men, they were together in the army, and Vic, the most restrained of the four, has listened quietly. While standing there, Vic remembers a moment of naval action, and he also recalls how he was at first mocked for his job, in the family undertaking business, but later this had been found useful for the carrying out of sea burials with some dignity. The visit requires them to climb a hill and Lenny complains predictably about this, and about the "fucking navy," "fucking army," and finally "fucking tourists." So how does this little excursion bear on the film as a whole? In one sense, the memorial is a last order for those who didn't make it, or a last attempt to impose a sort of order on the awful randomness of wartime deaths. The point of the wartime shots is to help us understand how life has shaped the men in the Merc, and the Memorial acts as focus for their recollections.

Wick's Farm

The next stopover happens when Vince pulls the car off the motorway and on to a dirt road that leads to a large muddy hillside field. The clever editing doesn't allow any further lead-in to this detour but cuts instead to Amy and Ray talking on the London Embankment and she utters the words "Wicks Farm," just as the Merc is coming to a halt. Vince offers no explanation for this as he gets out of the car and goes to scatter some of Jack's ashes there. Aggressive and never waiting for explanations, Lenny angrily calls Vince a "toe-rag," and, ex-boxer that he is, he knocks Vince down, shouting that "Jack's last orders have to be respected." In fact, this was the place where, in the hop-picking season before the war, Jack and Amy had first made love and their daughter June was conceived. When the punch-slinging with Lenny is done, Vince stands in the field, recalling a conversation with Jack about June who is "sort of yer sister" but not wholly so. This is where Vince learned the fact of his parents' death in a London doodlebug bombing and how Amy had rescued the baby Vince. When Jack came back from the war, there was Vince installed in the family. Jack has had a mentally disabled daughter he can hardly bear to contemplate and a son who was not really his son. Vince remembers saying to Jack, "You're not really my dad," and then scatters some of the ashes. The juxtaposition of the memory and the gesture watched by the three old friends is suddenly very moving in the intense conjunction of past and present. Vince is here carrying out Jack's last orders in a wholly personal way, one that brings him a real sense of reconciliation of his present and his past.

Canterbury

Back in the car, Vince and Lenny, having got rid of the effects of their muddy scuffle as best they can, there is then talk of Canterbury, and Ray says he's never been there. "Well, Canterbury doesn't have a race course does it?" is Lenny's inevitably needling reply. There are moments of rare beauty in the way the cathedral rears up before them. This has nothing to do with so-called "heritage" filmmaking; it is everything to do with a gnawing sense of mortality and eternity. Once inside the cathedral, Vince picks up a tourist brochure and, while he and Lenny and Vic walk around the glowing interior, Ray elects to sit quietly on a pew at the back. This is a place full of effigies of the famous (Thomas à Becket, for instance), a place that is concerned with marking and honoring the dead, and those so honored are there in compliance with someone's last orders. For Ray, kind and usually upbeat, it provides a time for reflection.

He's on this trip to do what Jack has asked, but he is also recalling the time he has spent in loving Jack's wife and, as Amy weeps at her recollections of the six weeks long ago when she let Ray love her, Ray sits quietly weeping in the cathedral. The mutuality of their tears gently hints at a possible future, when both have paid their dues to others, a future that may include a trip to Australia to visit Ray's daughter Susie, with whom he has been long out of touch. The film registers Ray's reflections of his and Amy's tentative relationship with discreet memory flashes, of how "we couldn't do it to Jack," and how, in Amy's words, "He [Jack] couldn't love June but he did love me." It's as though the cathedral has provided a perspective for considering the past in the light of the present—or, as Ray's words have it in the novel: "What's the lick and spittle of a human life against [the cathedral's] fourteen centuries?"[9]

ON TO MARGATE

The film starts in the Bermondsey pub where the four older men had used to gather and where they must routinely have responded to barman Bernie's request for last orders. It's fitting that the film's journey begins there and ends on windswept Margate pier, which we last saw in the bright sunshine of the youth of Jack and Amy. Talk about the journey and stopovers isn't meant to suggest that *Last Orders* is a picaresque tale with interesting encounters along the way. The four in the car on their way to carry out Jack's last orders meet no one along the way, apart from people serving them in pubs. These are lives that have been shaped by the Second World War, and on this journey some of the things and people who have mattered to them come unbidden to the surface of their minds. The important journey is, for each of them, the inner one, as the film's meditative tone makes us privy to what it means to each. What happens on this journey is that, through the play of memories and reminiscence, about a dozen interconnected lives are gradually teased out, allusively but with great evocative vividness. What is recalled of their lives isn't whipped up into major dramas; its importance is for the men to help settle within and between themselves, as the penultimate shot of the film suggests. As Roger Ebert's review summarized: "Many old secrets are revealed in the course of the journey, but they are not really what the movie is about. The details are not as important as the act of memory itself."[10]

Schepisi's cameraman, Brian Tufano, ends the film on the most eloquent shots of the four men standing on the edge of the pier as they discharge Jack's last orders. Somehow, the shots of the four from behind as they face out to sea where the ashes have drifted are invested with the most acute poignancy. Perhaps it's as if whatever tensions have been observed along the way these are now subsumed into this farewell gesture. When they move back to the car, talking of having a drink ("Jack would expect nothing less"), the camera settles on a long shot of the serene greyness of the sea. Schepisi has found a visual equivalent for the novel's account of the four finally reaching the jetty. It's "like all the while we've been teetering and tottering towards some edge, and now there ain't no more hanging back."[11]

TIME PASSING

Even the notion of retirement carries with it some sense of "last orders," the last that will be given or taken at least in working lives. Jack's decision to sell up the Dodds and Son butchery has a quality of acceptance of time's inexorable hand. He has wanted Vince to join him so as to carry on the name that Jack's father had established, but Vince is more interested in running a car yard, which he establishes with Ray's help. Not long after Jack has decided to sell, wanting to set up in a bungalow in Margate, he takes ill, and his next and final move is to the hospital. Lenny, the least successful of the four friends, and envious about this, still has to ply his business, but Ray is retired, more or less contented with his lot and with doing things to help those who need help. Only Vic is still in charge of his business, but his sons are ready to take it over when required, unlike Vince in relation to the Dodds butchery. Coming to the end of your working life isn't quite the same as last orders, but is perhaps not an uncommon step towards that finality.

The film gives a sure sense of the passage of time. It is never confusing as it makes its way from the present of the journey in the Merc or Amy's parallel bus trip to say goodbye to June to the recent past involving the progress of Jack's illness, to the much more distant past of the war years and others in between. That there is no confusion about the period in which the action is taking place at any given time is doubtless due to Schepisi's orchestration of the whole multilayered narrative, recalling his adroitness with *Six Degrees of Separation*. We know immediately where we are, or at least which tense we're in, whether the Merc is making its progress through the Kentish countryside, or whether we're in the memory sequences, or the inserts within these. That this is clear is also partly the work of the production and costume design, of lighting. and even of the hair and makeup stylists. All of these keep us mutely informed. The Margate of Jack and Amy's honeymoon is bathed in the sunlight of a season other than the bleak one of the men's return. The bright red lips of the wartime women and their rolled hairstyles have become subdued by the time they've reached middle age, and so have their clothes, with Amy, for instance, later wrapped in warm overcoats and a knitted hat. In Ray's case, encroaching baldness is a help in placing him in various decades. The fact that the main characters are played by different actors at earlier stages is, of course, the most obvious informant about period, but all those other aspects of filmmaking work to persuade us about the authenticity of the time and place in which they are set.

A major element of the film's skill in marking the passage of time is its cunning use of young actors to play the six leading roles in their twenties or earlier in Vince's case. For example, Vince (played by Stephen Cole, as a young man) has grown out of his 1960s ponytail and his shaggy 1970s locks by the time we see him behind the wheels of the Merc a couple of decades later. JJ Feild is a miraculously apt young Jack, not just because of his credible resemblance to a young Michael Caine but also because he catches Jack's easy assumption of authority in any situation. As for the young Lenny, he is played by David Hemmings's son, Nolan, so that the resemblance to the 1960s star is not surprising. It is enough to say that all the youthful versions of the carload, and of Amy and Jack, are plausible forerunners of those we see making their journeys to carry out last orders, and this feeds our belief in the pasts that have made them.

KEEPING THEM SORTED

In a narrative that ranges about in time and place, it is important for the film to find a secure parallel with the novel's creation of recognizable voices. Schepisi's choice of actors, both as the older and younger versions of the same character, is clearly important.

On the subject of the actors, *Last Orders*' starring cast is virtually a compendium of British male film acting over nearly half a century. The careers of Michael Caine, David Hemmings, and Tom Courtenay really got under way in the 1960s (see what happens to various kinds of heroes in late middle age—in film and life), Hoskins's from the early '80s and Winstone's from the '90s, with the great Helen Mirren's spanning over forty years. Arguably none has ever been better than here; between them, they are heartbreakingly real, utterly true to their characters, and to the film's large themes, which have to do with nothing less than what life is worth, and on what sort of terms it might mean most. Caine, Hemmings, and Courtenay are now all much associated with fresh impulses in British cinema from the 1960s onward. The actors carry the recent history of England on their faces and in their worn, upright postures. As the *New York Times* review noted about the actors: "That movie audiences have, over the years, watched them grow older, and may retain images of their younger, brasher selves, only deepens the sense of affectionate familiarity."[12]

Caine entered films in uncredited bits in 1950, was first noticed in *A Hill in Korea* in 1956, but came to prominence with a string of versatile displays in the mid '60s, memorably as a serial womanizer in, and as, *Alfie* (1966). Unlike many theatre-trained British actors, he gave an impression less of acting than of effortlessly *behaving* in whatever role he was cast in. Over the next forty-odd years, he acquired the sort of image that seemed in line with that Hollywood tradition of stars who often appeared to be doing nothing at all but left you utterly convinced about the lives they were enacting—or inhabiting. In *Last Orders*, his Jack rightly hovers over the whole film, whether he's there dominating the company in a pub or lying flat on his back in a hospital ward or when the chaps in the car are just talking about him. He is, to the life, the working-class man who has happily inherited his dad's butcher shop and is terse with his "son" Vince, who doesn't want to maintain the line in this matter. He is loud and confident most of the time, and this makes the more affecting those moments when, for instance, he is concerned about "seeing Amy right" after he is dead.

The smoothly good-looking Hemmings was in films from 1954, at the age of thirteen, but finally made his presence felt in a big way in Michelangelo Antonioni's spectacularly successful art-house hit, *Blow-Up* in 1966, as the modish London photographer who thinks he's stumbled on something suspicious. He worked steadily until his death in 2003, increasingly in character roles as his youthful looks gave way to somewhat pudgy middle-age, a condition that suited him admirably to the role of the stroppy, envious, and disappointed Lenny. He has a grudge against Jack's "son," Vince, who had once got Lenny's daughter pregnant, and he blames Vince for her having then married a guy who is now in jail. Hemmings brings to his playing of Lenny a bitter edginess that is kept in check only by the odd pint or, at the end, by the quartet's discharging of Jack's last orders as a group effort.

There was something pinched and inward-looking about the young Courtenay as he endured and made us understand *The Loneliness of the Long-Distance Runner* (1962) and the sense of entrapment felt by *Billy Liar!* (1963). He was one of the "icons," as they say, of the British New Wave, which produced a newly proletarian set of stars who had little in common with the previous traditions of British leading men. Like Caine, he came from a modest working-class background, and over the next half-century he was persistently at work, across a wide social range, on stage, screen, and television. His originally rather glum appearance had settled by the time of *Last Orders* (and by *Quartet*, a decade later) into a quiet contentment that is perfectly adapted to the character of Vic, the undertaker. He brings to the role the sense of a man at peace with himself, and the touch of dignity that the occasion calls for. Of the four older men, he is perhaps the one most satisfied with the cards that life has dealt him, and in the visit to the War Memorial, Courtenay brings just a flicker of something still stirring beneath the calm facade.

Bob Hoskins, a little younger than Caine and Courtenay but the same age as Hemmings, seems to belong to a different generation of British film. He did quite a bit of television in the '70s, but his film career only took off in 1980 when he played the wealthy gangster Harold Shand in *The Long Good Friday*. From then on, he became perhaps the major character star in British films, with side excursions into big-budget Hollywood jobs. There is something quintessentially English and stubbornly working-class about him, and his short, sturdy frame was ideally suited to the role of Ray, the most obviously benign of the *Last Orders* guys. He can play Ray as Amy's temporary lover without somehow compromising Ray's core of decency.

The youngest of the four on the road, Vince is played by Ray Winstone. Also from a working-class background and with several boxing championships to his name, he was active in film and television from the late '70s, but came into his own as the hard man of British films in the '90s in such rigorous fare as *Nil by Mouth* (1997) and *The War Zone* (1999). Everything about his physical presence—his stance, the way he wears his bulk (and his camel-hair coat)—feeds impressively into how he brings Vince to life. He suggests a man capable of physical violence, though this is only called into play when he hits back at Lenny in the hopfield. He also suggests a man who is perhaps not as sure of himself and his place in the world as we may at first believe.

I stress the way these five actors represent decades-long strands of British filmmaking, because *Last Orders* is so patently an actors' film and because of the echoes they bring with them. As for Helen Mirren, she seems so much a star of today, appearing in film after film, that it is hard to accept that she first appeared, uncredited, in a Norman Wisdom farce, *Press for Time*, in 1966. She has contrived to be a major star without surrendering her credentials as a major actress. As Amy, she has been prepared to subdue her natural sexiness and glamour in the interests of playing a middle-aged, then elderly housewife with a daughter who still doesn't know her after her fifty years of devoted and painful solicitude. While the men in the Merc are calling up their memories, Amy is quietly locked into hers on the top of the red London bus.

...

From his earliest films, Schepisi has shown a remarkable flair as a director of actors, somehow allowing them to draw on their own personae while at the same time creating a feeling for how they inhabit the world of the film. *Last Orders* is perhaps his major achievement in this respect, though several other of his films come near to contesting such an accolade. Certainly Swift's novel gave plenty of material for actors to draw on, and they have repaid this with a remarkable ensemble of interlocking lives. And the film as a whole warrants the encomium of the critic who eulogized it as "an unsentimental, witty, star-studded, unpatronizing, intelligent, adult—and cinematic—British film."[13] However, some US critics were less enthusiastic. For instance, the *San Francisco Chronicle* reviewer felt that "this is an enervated, overly muted drama that should have been a lot livelier, considering the terrific cast"[14]. However, the *Rolling Stone* critic, also finding it "gorgeously acted," summed up by saying: "With all the back and forth, Schepisi succeeds admirably in holding an emotional through-line. The film is a bawdy delight that also stays alert to the petty lies and jealousies that can rupture a friendship."[15] I'd argue that this latter assessment offers an astute appraisal of Schepisi's structural control and his humane concern for the complex lives revealed.

Chapter Eight

IN THE NEW CENTURY

In the 2000s, Schepisi's speed of delivery may have slowed somewhat, but he turned for the first time to a major US television production (*Empire Falls*, 2005) and returned to Australia to film Patrick White's *The Eye of the Storm* (2011). However, before these came one of his most problematic features, *It Runs in the Family*, the incidental pleasures of which never quite add up to a satisfying whole.

IT RUNS IN THE FAMILY (2003)

Like the remarkable *Six Degrees of Separation* ten years earlier, *It Runs in the Family* offers more exploration of family conflict in the setting of metropolitan New York. This time, though, "family" not only refers to the fictitious upper-middle-class Jewish Grombergs, but hovering over the whole film is the aura of the real-life Douglas family: Kirk, ex-wife Diana, son Michael, and grandson Cameron. As a result, it is almost impossible not to ponder while watching the film how far real-life drama has been filtered into the fiction. To misquote a recent film title, "not all is true," but the effect of possible parallels does become distracting. As one reviewer wrote: "Throughout the movie you can feel the actors" off-screen relationships resonating with their performances and enriching them immeasurably";[1] and another felt that "as the film progresses there are intriguing moments of parallel between life and art."[2]

How Did It Come About?

An account of the film's origins and the involvement of the Douglas family members is to be found in Schepisi's 2003 interview with Tom

Ryan.[3] As with *Last Orders*, its immediate predecessor, Schepisi again takes on the kinds of tensions and conflicts that family life can give rise to. In setting up the film, he had to take into account the fact that in 1996 Kirk Douglas suffered a stroke as a result of a helicopter accident, that the role of his son in the film, to be played by Michael, seemed seriously underwritten, and that Michael's son, Cameron, had almost no acting experience. In fact, "in order for Cameron to take part in the film, Michael insisted he spend a few months studying with a top acting coach, then he actually had to screen test for the picture."[4] Furthermore, would it be easy to accommodate Kirk's long-since ex-wife, Diana, in the role of his on-screen wife? Both Kirk and Michael "had long wanted to do something together, something they could share as father and son in a business they both understand extremely well."[5] However, none of the possibilities raised ever seemed quite right until young New York screenwriter Jesse Wigutow came up with the draft of a screenplay called *It Runs in the Family*, though the "family" wasn't originally intended to be the Douglases—and it is arguable that it ended up being "quite right."

Though the viewer may feel some confusion between the relationships among the real-life Douglas family and the on-screen Grombergs, Schepisi is clear that this was not at all an original intention. He explained: "A lot of people misunderstand this. Most of what's in the film was written way before the Douglases ever saw it. The whole part for Cameron is completely as it was before any Douglas became involved. Much of the part for Kirk . . . was written way before Kirk Douglas ever came into consideration. The only part that's dramatically changed is, in fact, Michael's."[6] The mention of Michael refers to the rewriting involved in bolstering his role in the interests of making clearer the relationship between the film's father and son, Mitchell and Alex Gromberg. Michael, producer as well as star, was also apparently nervous about his father's state of health.

About the Douglases' participation, Schepisi insists that "every one of them understood that what they were doing was playing fictional characters, and like all good actors, they drew on themselves, their own experience and research. In this case, the research was very close to their own lives. . . . But none of them made the mistake of confusing it with real life."[7] However, while accepting Schepisi's account, the inter-generational parallels can be disconcerting to the viewer with any knowledge of the Douglas family, though this need not weigh against the film's narrative potential and the pleasures offered, even if other aspects of the film may do so.

The Grombergs Get Together

There is so much talk about the Douglas family and how it came to participate in *It Runs in the Family* and the kinds of parallels between them and the film's protagonists, the Grombergs, that it involves an almost-conscious effort to return to the film as the fictional work it is—and, as Schepisi said, one that was conceived prior to the involvement of the Douglases. In some ways, it seems one of his least successful films, inclined to be straggling rather than carefully structured, but hardly deserving the put-down of "vacuous vanity project," in the words of one reviewer.[8]

Perhaps the underlying motif of three generations of inter- and intra-relationships at each level, each undergoing stress and grief in varying degrees, is meant to hold the film together, to give it an underlying structure, but in fact this doesn't quite work. This is not to say that there aren't moments of wit and perception but, instead, that these positive qualities are noted in sequences that fail to build the expected momentum.

The first "movement" (though that term sounds too structured in the context) is towards the family gathering for a Passover Seder dinner. By the time this is under way, the film has introduced the family via photographs and the metropolitan setting of city streets and high-rise apartment blocks, and the Manhattan skyline, the latter of which recalls its more expressive usage in *Six Degrees*. This is seen behind the credits while accompanied by Paul Grabowsky's jaunty score. In immediate post-credits, Mitch (Kirk Douglas) is depicted as being "in remarkable shape," a year after his stroke, with a doctor promising him "a few good years left." In successive brief episodes, we see: a young boy Eli Gromberg (Rory Culkin) molding odd shapes in class; his psychotherapist mother, Rebecca (Bernadette Peterson), phoning her attorney husband, Alex (Michael Douglas), to remind him that his parents are coming to dinner; their older son, Asher (Cameron Douglas), slouching in a university class where there is talk of anti-Semitism; and Mitch calling on his demented older brother, Stephen (Mark Hammer).

Then frustrations and oopses set in. Eli and his friends are set upon by other kids because of conflicting views on Abby (Irina Gorovala), whom Eli has eyed with interest in class. Asher, drawn to an attractive girl called Peg (Michelle Monaghan), has failed to collect his grandmother, Evelyn (Diana Douglas), at a dialysis clinic. Alex, doing volunteer work in a soup kitchen, has succumbed to the enthusiastic sexual advances of a co-worker, Suzie (Sarita Choudhury). The reason for giving all the foregoing detail is partly to suggest that the narrative may be heading to some sort of turning point, but equally, from a critical point of view, it highlights one of the film's problems. That is, the film is overcrowded with snippets of information, which can sometimes give it a ragged appearance, and at the same time not enough detail to ensure a viewer's engagement with the range of characters and their situations. However, it may be only fair to quote Schepisi's own comment on this opening series of episodes: "The whole point of the first sequence is to slowly take you through who all these people are and bring them together."[9]

Family gatherings in films (perhaps also in life?) are almost inevitably the occasion for conflicts to surface, and up to a point this is the case here. Asher saunters in to dinner unapologetically late, just as his father is snapping at Mitch, and Evelyn tells Alex he should be more tolerant of his ailing father. An exterior shot of the apartment building reveals the site of the gathering bathed in soft light, at odds with what has been revealed of the tensions within. Reference to that long shot recalls how much more effectively *Six Degrees* made the New York location work: in the earlier film, it seemed almost a participant in the action involving its upper-middle-class characters, whereas in *It Runs in the Family* it emerges as little more than "setting." And when the camera prowls Mitch's apartment, it also reminds one of how Ian Baker's camera wound its way through the Kittredges' spacious quarters (also in Patrizia von Brandenstein's eloquent production design) to much more significant effect in establishing important aspects of their lives than is the case in the later film.

It is not the aim of this study to trawl through the whole film in the kind of detail given in relation to the above early episodes, nor to imply that there is no more to it than an underdeveloped succession of mini-dramas, though one reviewer claimed that the plot is "so jammed with events, disputes, tragedies and revelations that the most serious matters don't seem to receive enough attention."[10] While there may be some truth in this negative assessment, there are also occasions in the film when Schepisi, working from Jesse Wigutow's admittedly crowded screenplay, strikes responsive chords about these interlocking family tensions.

Three Generations

Despite some sense of the overcrowding of character and incident, *It Runs in the Family* still contrives to make at least intermittent drama of the generational conflicts and stresses that account for its narrative trajectory. There are, for instance, un-emphatically but clearly made contrasts in the bedroom episodes of each generation. The two young sons, drug-dealing teenager Asher and karate-champ kid Eli, will have moments with their girlfriends, to be considered shortly. There is genuine affection in the sequence in which Evelyn turns on Bobby Darin's singing "You'll Never Know . . ." and insists to Mitch that he stop watching the Yankees on TV and that they dance to the song. Shortly afterwards, when she has lain down and he again watches and then turns off the TV, he finds her dead on the bed. Their long marriage was not without its spiky moments, but this episode makes clear that there was also a long-lasting love that had survived these.

At Evelyn's funeral, Alex says in his eulogy, "One look from her, she knew what the truth was," and watching him coldly is Rebecca, who has shortly before found Suzie's panties in his coat pocket (how they got there is not made clear) and knows now she cannot expect to glean the truth by looking at *him*. In what may be the film's finest performance, Bernadette Peters finds a touching complexity in Rebecca's situation here. During the funeral, she has repressed her feelings in the interests of old Mitch's needs, but in the next bedroom scene, she will burst out angrily at Alex's duplicity (he insists, "It's nothing"), and he will take his pillows to make up a bed on the sofa.

When Alex is subsequently driving Mitch to the place where he first met Evelyn, Mitch says, "I can hardly breathe without her," and is eyed by Alex, who has messed up *his* marriage and who gets no comfort from his father. The awkwardness at the heart of this scene is handled so well, with subtlety and pathos (but not sentimentality), that one could wish for more of such qualities in the course of the film. When Mitch tells Alex, "You're a much better father than I was," Alex, laughing, replies, "You didn't exactly set the bar that high," adding that he would have liked "just a little bit of approval." As Stephen Holden's review wrote, "The two stars have made no secret that their relationship has weathered its share of strife,"[11] and Roger Ebert's less-positive review also allowed that "the film is certainly courageous in the way it deals with Kirk Douglas's stroke, Michael Douglas's infidelity and the drug problems of a son played by Cameron Douglas."[12]

When it comes to the third generation, there is still the prospect of personally difficult times ahead, and one of the film's strengths is that there is never a suggestion of a feel-good ending aimed at keeping audiences happy. Asher is a young guy who sometimes seems to be slouching through life, trying to write a play to be called *Family Jewels*, but uncertain what he wants: writing? music? sex? As to the latter, the very attractive Peg, who later arrives at his messy room, has been a willing participant, but he will not long after get arrested for his dealing in home-grown marijuana, prompting Peg to have nothing more to do with him. Perhaps there is a more positive note struck in young Eli's interest in the schoolgirl called Abby, with a ring in her nose. He fights back successfully (and a shade improbably) when thugs set upon them, this subsequently leading Abby to ask him: "How come you haven't tried to kiss me?" "No thank you," he says, and then: "Okay." One critic claimed that "the film is most successful in dealing with the awkwardness of Eli's move into adolescence,"[13] and Rory Culkin's Eli strikes the right balance of gaucherie and aggression.

At the other far end of the generational ladder, Mitch's demented brother, Stephen (Mark Harmer), who has lost any sense of reality, dies. This gives rise to one of the film's most improbable moments: Mitch and Alex take his body to a forest lake, where they place him on a boat, push this out on to the lake and set fire to it. (Could this have been intended as an echo of Kirk Douglas's 1958 film *The Vikings*?) Mitch claims that this is what Stephen would have wanted; Alex thinks it's mad and that they could go to jail as a result.

Well, they don't, and the film makes its way to its compromised ending. It doesn't engage in a family hug, either physical or metaphorical. Asher weeps as he talks of Peg and of having screwed up at school; Rebecca won't have Alex back in her bed; and in the last moments, both Mitch and Alex have been relegated to couches, where Alex tells his father he is leaving the family firm. As the admiring critic Stephen Holden wrote: "Although the Grombergs' interlocking personal dramas ultimately bring them somewhat closer, the screenplay offers no pat resolutions to any of their problems."[14] But there are imagistic juxtapositions and echoes that go some distance to holding the film together. For example, from the brief episode in which Mitch and Evelyn enter their "usual" restaurant and order their "usual" dinner, the film cuts to Rebecca and Alex at their dinner where they exchange wedding anniversary gifts. Near the end there is a poignant echo when Rebecca, having expelled Alex from their bed, arranges his pillows as a sort of barrier to his presence, recalling Mitch's rearranging of Evelyn's pillows after her death so as to remind him of a once-loved presence. If the film lacks a tight structure, it is not without such rewarding moments.

A Mixed Reception

Virtually all the critical responses to the film—and, presumably, those of most audiences—took into consideration parallels with the real-life Douglas family, and given the casting, this would be hard to avoid. Ebert may well have been right when, disclaiming knowledge of how accurately the film drew on the actual history, he summed up: "My guess is that most of the facts are different and a lot of the emotions are the same."[15] Assessing the film from such a point of view, and this is no doubt the fairest such, there is still a good deal of wit and sympathetic understanding in the unfolding of the crowded scenario.

In the US, Holden's review is one of the most positive, praising Jesse Wigutow's screenplay "as one of those marvels of economy, idiomatic facility and well-chosen detail that knows exactly when to cut away from a scene without grinding it into your face" and how "Fred Schepisi's direction finds a comfortable balance between comedy and clear-eyed realism. Over and over, the movie flirts with sentimentality, then dances away from it."[16] Up to a point, one can go along with these views, though the reference to the screenplay's not "grinding it in your face" can sometimes seem at odds with over-explicit comments on the order of: "We're a family.... We've got to figure this out together." However, even when it smacks of the didactic, there is still something engaging in the way the film is prepared to leave matters unresolved when those matters seem too messy for easy resolution, and Schepisi's direction does find credible compromise here. Elsewhere in the US, the film received Ebert's measured judgment, several times referred to above, and a surprisingly vicious put-down in the *San Francisco Times*, describing it as "a vanity piece" and "achingly long and pointless, . . . a movie about family that's dishonest in its presentation of every relationship."[17] What precisely does "dishonest" mean here? The film may have faults, but dishonesty scarcely seems to be one of them.

The film attracted a similarly negative review in the UK, where the BBC dismissed it as "an inferior clone of the Fonda family weepie 'On Golden Pond,'"[18] and *Sight & Sound*, less dismissive, and allowing that "Schepisi steers clear of mawkishness," nevertheless felt that "he never really succeeds in making the audience care for the characters or their various plights."[19] In Australia, *Urban Cinefile* reviewer, Andrew L. Urban praised "Schepisi's ability to weave them ['the four key relationships'] together into a coherent and meaningful picture," though his colleague, Louise Keller, while praising the performances, felt that "it plays out pleasantly with some well observed moments, but never totally satisfies."[20] Another Australian reviewer, under the feebly punning title, "A Relative Flop," rather brutally described it as "This syrupy, sitcom-ish gloop" and, as for a bringing together of the Douglas clan, found "that there is nothing much to celebrate in the way of entertaining filmmaking here."[21]

Perhaps no other of Schepisi's films has been subject to such a range of critical opinion. In the light of its real-life parallels, it was perhaps a contentious project, and even Schepisi himself had some apprehensions about it. The film undoubtedly has a cluttered screenplay, but, whatever reservations one may feel as it hurries from one moment of tension to another, there are still rewarding touches of wit and the realities of human experience—of families, whether real-life or fictional.

EMPIRE FALLS

Could a pun have been intended? The title of the film and the antecedent novel could almost be seen as a part-summary of the narrative: the town that provides its setting is called Empire Falls, and it could be said that for much of its length we are watching the fall of the Whiting family's empire in this town. The retrieval of its status is really little more than a statement at the end.

Small Screen/Big Film

Adapting Richard Russo's 483-page, Pulitzer Prize-winning novel[22] must have offered a demanding task to the filmmaker. Schepisi, whose only major television work *Empire Falls* is, claims that he shot it "as a film . . . I wasn't shooting it as a series of parts . . . it was made to be viewed in one sitting."[23] What materialized was a three-and-a-quarter hour film, which was subsequently divided into two "Parts," thus constituting a miniseries of sorts, each Part being divided into four "Chapters," each of the latter complete with its title. Watching the two Parts, however, seems like a very different experience from the more usual miniseries experience in which each episode has to move towards an ending that keeps audiences eager for the next. The idea for the film came to Schepisi through Paul Newman's agent, and Newman became an executive producer on the project, as did Schepisi.

Another Adaptation

Almost half of Schepisi's films have been derived from literary works, both plays (*Six Degrees of Separation*, *Plenty*, *Roxanne*) and novels from *The Chant of Jimmie Blacksmith* to *Eye of the Storm* (2011, his last in this mode), and he has persistently shown himself adept at making "something new" from an earlier work. In this process, he has also had considerable experience in working with some very notable authors, such David Hare on *Plenty*, John Guare on *Six Degrees*, and Graham Swift on *Last Orders*. As he said:

> I've been lucky enough to work with some great writers, like David Hare, Tom Stoppard, John Guare and Richard Russo. You can really work with them: they're not at all defensive as lesser writers can be. When you say: "I don't get this? What's wrong here?" they can articulate for you what you haven't seen—or, if not, they stop and think, and you might make a suggestion and they'll take it up, and make it their own again, or they might show you that that's not the problem. Then you get a really creative collaboration and you have to disembowel it and then come back to it to see it from their point of view, until you know it inside out.[24]

He always felt it important to respect the earlier text while at the same time making it a work of his own. On *Empire Falls*, he recalled that "Richard Russo and I did a lot of work on it," this "work" including his saying to Russo: "Do me a favor. Read your book again, but don't read the first two chapters and see how the information contained in them comes out through the rest."[25] When one listens to the conversation between the two in the audio commentary over the nearly muted DVD of the film, it becomes clear how important this kind of collaboration was to the film's outcome.[26]

Taking the opposite line and rereading those first two Chapters, one senses what Schepisi may have had in mind: they are apt to spell out in advance matters that, at least in a film version, may be left to emerge in the audio-visual imagery in which the interaction of characters with each other and, indeed, with the community must emerge. Film *shows* what often a novel will *tell* and, admirable as Russo's novel is, in these early Chapters there is more "information" given than may be needed.

In the screenplay, credited solely to Russo himself, it seems that the author has taken heed of Schepisi's suggestion. The first Chapter in Part 1 of the film is the longest in the two Parts and is entitled "In which we learn that anything is possible." Even before this title is announced, there have been sepia shots of Indians who "took land seriously till wiped out by war, class, Christianity and other European diseases," large red crosses over the sepia photos signifying the end of the indigenous ways. There are also images of the river, earlier used for logging, now for chemical and other waste disposal, and color comes in to depict the "town that sprang up: Empire Falls, Maine, "no better or worse than other mill towns," as the narrator (Larry Pine) informs us.

A Schepisi Film—For Whichever Medium

In Chapter 1, Schepisi, in the wake of his own advice to Russo, exercises his characteristic skill in dealing with a diversity of character and with shifts between past and present, in the process demonstrating the filmmaker's preference for showing rather than telling. Whereas the opening half-hour of *It Runs in the Family* can seem somewhat overcrowded and directionless as it sets the various family elements in motion, this is not the case with Chapter 1 of *Empire Falls*. Here, he establishes the sense of a community—business, now in a state of decline, church, also looking run down in its building and in its key personnel, and school, as well as individual dwellings—and gradually immerses us in the diversity of a town that has seen its better days. But that sense of community so effortlessly established has predecessors in such disparate Schepisi productions as *Roxanne* and *Six Degrees*. As in such earlier works, Baker's camera observantly prowls the town at large and investigates the interiors, skillfully differentiated in Stuart Wurzel's production design (all underpinned by Paul Grabowsky's reflective score), for example, in the streets, the drab factory exteriors, Mrs. Whiting's grand house with its riverside gazebo, and Miles Roby's cramped quarters above the Empire Grills, which he manages for "the lady" (i.e., Mrs. Whiting). And there are intervening images of the Knox River, which recall Russo's contrasting view of "what water wanted to do was flow downhill" and how its "meandering intentions were thwarted"[27] by man's intervention.

Throughout this study, there have been recurring references to Schepisi's responsiveness to shifting times and places, and this is again evident in how he sets so much information before us in Chapter 1. Some of the film's key relationships are set in motion, starting with a present-day scene between the good-natured Miles (Ed Harris) and his cadging, alcoholic father Max (a much-aged Paul Newman) and with later flashbacks to ten-year-old Miles (Miles Chandler) and his, mother Grace (Robin Wright Penn), vacationing at Martha's Vineyard when Max had been in jail, and ending with Max standing in the rain at the grave of his long-dead wife. There is also what amounts to a brief history of the town in a series of sepia shots, while in Miles's restaurant a man opines that "things could go well for this town again."

The past, the present, and a possible future are all conjured up in this Chapter: there is more going on than suggested here, the examples chosen merely to stress again the narrative fluidity which is one of Schepisi's strengths. Actually film, by its very nature, is more at ease with this sort of fluidity than the novel, and in the case of Russo's *Empire Falls*, his method of taking us back into the past is to offer slabs of text in italics, which can seem a bit cumbersome on occasion.

This opening Chapter not merely gives us the feeling of a community, much of it in decline, or of Schepisi's skill with time-shifts. The film's first Chapter also initiates a concern with life's possibilities, as did such earlier titles as *The Devil's Playground* and *Six Degrees*. What, for instance, are the prospects for seemingly decent, intelligent, but not forceful Miles, or for his estranged wife, Janine (Helen Hunt), as she contemplates remarriage with Walt Cameau (Dennis Farina), who runs a health club, or for Callahan's bar, where Janine's mother, Bea (Estelle Parsons), works, or for the implacable matriarch Mrs. Whiting (Joanne Woodward)? In terms of narrative impulse, a good deal has been set in motion by the end of this Chapter, without any sense of the film's simply darting from one situation to another: the interaction of individual and community will be at the heart of the film's holding power. One reviewer of the novel wrote: "Russo's tale takes on the structure of an unfolding series of interlocking secrets."[28] Invoking the resources of cinema, Schepisi pursues a comparable narrative goal.

So What Happens Now?

The voice-over that initiates Chapter 1 goes on to inform us that Empire Falls was populated by European immigrants such as the Robys (the Indian natives having been dismissed in sepia shots of long ago). However, the Roby family, of whom we first see father Max and son Miles in conflict over Miles's car, may have "built Empire Falls but they didn't own it." The unseen voice goes on to say: "The family that owned the town for more than a century was the Whitings, who owned all that was worth owning." Out of context, this may sound like a too-explicit account of the underlying tensions of the town—not to mention the film. Instead, though, it raises audience anticipation about the history of the town as it seems to be rotting away and of the powers behind it and those at their mercy.

The brief sepia history of the town gives way to spotlighting Mrs. Whiting, who lives surrounded by portraits of her predecessors some of whom she recalls with waspish utterance. When Miles visits her, at her invitation, she has a "surprise" for him: his father has been asking for money, and she describes Max as "a pain in the ass"; she also wants Miles to run for mayor, though, as she says, her influence can extend no further than urging him; and she wants a further business meeting with Miles. In their scenes together, they hint at the kind of manipulation of the town's affairs she may be willing to engage in and at the tolerant Miles's mixture of deference and astuteness. Woodward and Harris charge their scenes together with an apt blending of the said and the unsaid, perfectly capturing the "major theme of Old Money warping the destiny of ordinary working people."[29]

Though the relative influences of the Roby and Whiting families— the former initially—the latter far-ranging, may account for much of the town's life and the film's narrative interest, there is also a good deal going on in, and questions raised about, personal matters in the opening Chapter. A flashback has informed us about Max's having been in jail, but not why, or what caused his marriage to Miles's mother Grace to fail in the years leading up to her early death, or what has brought him to the state of irresponsible old age in which we first viewed him.

Similarly, what has led to the breakdown of Miles and Janine's marriage is glimpsed in a sequence in which she confronts him about why he didn't love her, claiming that he "never said anything." What might have seemed like spelling out the state of play between them becomes, in the interaction of Harris and Hunt's playing, the dramatization of two people trying to know what to say and feel, his quiet restraint trying to deal with her forthrightness. Though Harris's Miles is the film's key protagonist, it is not ungenerous to Hunt's Janine, and the tensions between them are strengthened by the matter of their teenage daughter, Tick (Danielle Panabaker). We have seen Miles's restrained but obvious devotion to Tick when she arrived at the restaurant; now, later, he claims that he wants custody of her. There is a firmness here in his claim that implies that there is more to him than the unemphatic, good-natured fellow we have seen.

Russo's screenplay is proficient in inciting such viewer curiosity, and, in Schepisi's way of hitting on the essence of various encounters, in gratifying this. Among the sharply differentiated characters who are introduced in this opening Chapter is Miles's brother David (Aidan Quinn), whose mother's last words to him were: "Look after your brother." This causes us to ponder the present-day dynamics of relations between the two. And that last shot of Max standing in the rain by the grave of his wife Grace, then turning to observe the grave of C. B. Whiting, Francine's husband, implies in a fleeting glance that there may subsequently be grounds for this cutting from one image to another, for some connection to be revealed later.

And Later

As was not always the case with *It Runs in the Family*'s opening sequences, when the links between this and that image or event and those that preceded or followed it were sometimes less than clear, Chapter 1 of *Empire Falls* excites anticipation for further developments on both individual and community levels. The town may be dominated by Mrs. Whiting, and we shall see some of the effects of this, but the *film* will be dominated by the usually quietly spoken Miles. It is the character of Miles and how he influences and/or responds to changing circumstances that provide the film's core, and, in Ed Harris's Miles, Schepisi has secured one of the great performances of his career, already strewn with the likes of Stockard Channing's Ouisa in *Six Degrees* or those of the male ensemble of *Last Orders*.

I have spent so much space on Chapter 1 to suggest how it sets in motion the key lines of development of the rest of the film. Chapter 2—"The surprise"—opens with Miles's arrival at Mrs. Whiting's house, where he is greeted by her crippled daughter Cindy, with whom he appears to share a mutually friendly feeling. Or is it more than this? The film doesn't dwell on this now, and Miles is summoned by a bell to Mrs. Whiting's riverside gazebo. Here, after a discussion about Miles's running of the Empire Grills restaurant where brother David's menu is proving a hit, she claims: "I know you better than you know yourself." Again a query is set up for the viewer: what exactly does she know "better"? They have been discussing the "hard life" of Miles's mother. In a flashback to his boyhood holiday in Martha's Vineyard, Miles, sitting in his car reflecting on Mrs. Whiting's words, recalls how he, as a child, saw his mother embracing Charlie Mayne (Philip Seymour Hoffman). Chapter 2 then ends on a long shot of Mrs. Whiting's watching—watching what? Only towards the end of Chapter 7 ("White limos"), when Charlie/C. B. Whiting returns home after ten years and shoots himself, can we guess what might have been preoccupying Mrs. Whiting, after the talk with Miles about his mother. The intricacy of the film's links never seems merely the product of an overly convoluted narrative, but, rather, of the way thoughts and feelings and events are so intimately intertwined.

It is impossible, tempting though the prospect is, to trawl through the three-hour miniseries in this way, but it is enough to say that nothing seems wasted or irrelevant. A comment by Schepisi in the audio commentary over Chapter 5 hits on a crucial matter in the depiction of individuals and their relationships with each other and with the community. In conversation with Russo, he says: "One of the difficulties of film is showing the interior life and what someone is thinking."[30] He illustrates his point by referring to the scene in which Miles and cop Jimmy Minty (Michael Fichtner), who nurses a class-based resentment of Miles, are seated in Minty's car. There is tension between the two men, registered not so much in dialogue as in the way the camera moves from face-to-face recording reactions, spoken and unspoken, and reminding one of how Baker had achieved a similar effect in *Last Orders*. And shortly after this, there is a memorable cut between the boy Miles running puzzled after his mother and the older Miles poised on a stepladder and clearly, in the close-up of his face, recalling something significant to him. This is perhaps in relation to his mother, seen in expressive close-ups in the memory sequences as she walks to—and leans over the railing of—a bridge, where for a moment the boy fears for her safety. There is a brief shot of a poster which announces "Leaving Empire Falls," as if articulating the possibility that the older Miles remembers now (in relation to his mother's turmoil), whereas such a connection might not have appeared to the boy. In other words, film has its ways of suggesting "the interior life," even when it is leaving the audience to speculate on its exact nature, and this is a film that depends greatly on what goes on in the minds of its characters, and especially of its protagonist Miles, who emerges as a man of more thought than words.

Before leaving the two-part film's structural framework, I list all the Chapter headings (including those previously named) to suggest its overall narrative or thematic movement.

Part 1

Chapter 1—In which we learn that anything is possible
Chapter 2—The surprise
Chapter 3—Ties that bind
Chapter 4—Homecoming

Part 2

Chapter 5—The kind of attitude that leads to things
Chapter 6—Big doings
Chapter 7—White limos
Chapter 8—Boats against the current
Epilogue—How things turn out

This listing points to a kind of reflectiveness that binds the film's preoccupation with how personal matters interweave with broader perspectives.

Who's Who—And Why?

Empire Falls is essentially a film of crucial relationships, which often spill out over the wider spectrum of the small-town community at large. It is a place where everybody knows—or knows about—everyone else. It might have seemed overcrowded, but that the core figure of Miles, in Ed Harris's flawlessly subtle playing, holds it together and leads us to reflect on how and when these relationships have formed, what binds them or fragments them, and how they are reflected in the mosaic of the town's life. In this matter, Schepisi has the advantage of a stellar cast, all of whom seem more concerned with their roles in the film's overall texture than with projecting star personae.

Over the course of the two-part film, and over a period of many years, those earlier ones memorably glimpsed in flashbacks, Miles is seen to be engaged in at least a half-dozen relationships of varying degrees of complexity. Some of these have been adverted to above: for instance, his edgy dealings with Mrs. Whiting, who addresses him as "dear boy," while seeking to maintain a strict control over him in business and other matters, such as his management of Empire Grills and his wish to extend this. Miles knows he is being managed, and Harris's way in close-up of quietly suggesting this knowledge to us while not letting it be apparent to Mrs. Whiting, and in Woodward's deceptively gracious exterior when the camera moves in on her, account for some sharply suggestive moments. And while in the Whiting mansion, Miles displays a friendly concern—perhaps something more—for Mrs. Whiting's crippled daughter Cindy (Kate Burton), whose mother (in a younger incarnation played by Carey Lowell) has told him what a comfort he is to Cindy. We later see Miles with Cindy at a football match where he solicitously retrieves her walking stick under the grandstand. The film feels no need to tie up this relationship, and there is, curiously perhaps, no sense of frustration about this. Some situations, it seems to imply, don't necessarily require narrative closure.

Miles's other key relationships are those with his estranged wife Janine, with his mother who died young and confused the boy by seeming to prefer Charlie to her husband Max, with whom, as seen above, he has a difficult father-son set-up, with the brother Aidan, whose culinary skills benefit the restaurant, with police officer Jimmy Minty, who has issues with Miles, and, very important as striking an unambiguously positive note, with his daughter Tick. "Positive" in the sense that the devotion between them is unquestioned, but Tick's own experience of life in Empire Falls is far from being merely straightforward. She has had to deal with the breakdown of her parents' marriage, and the camera draws in on her unhappy face at her mother's wedding to flashy gym owner Walt Cameau. And horrific is her experience at school when the disturbed boy, Voss, whom she has supported against youthful bullies, returns one day with a gun and shoots many of the students, but there is reality and warmth in Tick's moments with her father.

Relationships are at the heart of the film, and Schepisi, working from Russo's screenplay and with a very gifted cast, focuses on how these work—or fail to work—and how they connect with the wider community of Empire Falls. Miles has had a troubled background. Not only did he observe his mother's relationship with Charlie Mayne, but he had not finished his college education when she became ill. Everything we learn about Miles seems to feed into that quiet, almost stoical acceptance of what life has handed him. In his one burst of violent action, when he lashes out physically at Jimmy Minty, Harris makes us see a man who had just been pushed beyond what essential decency can handle.

Violence is not depicted as part of the everyday life of Empire Falls, and, in the few occasions when it surfaces, it shocks with the possible reverberations: the schoolroom massacre, the Miles/Minty fisticuffs, and the images of the gazebo-set suicide of the returning Charlie (Mayne) Whiting and, near the film's end, of his widow's death in the swollen river. A quiet irony may be felt in the death of the string-pulling Mrs. Whiting just as the town is once again on the brink of a new prosperity, with a computer warehouse, impressive houses built, and salmon again in the river. The recurring images of the river, sometimes serene, sometimes polluted, the setting for moments of serenity or threat and the Chapter 8 title, "Boats against the current," point to its thematic importance as distinct from mere setting.

There is so much more one might discuss about this film that there is almost a danger of wallowing in its quiet complexities. Schepisi, as he has said, shot it as a film, and, in watching or writing about it, it never seems like a television miniseries. It is vast in its scope but meticulous in its unobtrusive evocation of a network of lives that so often feel like "boats against the current." *Variety*'s somewhat grudging review concluded by saying "the tendency is to forgive 'Empire Falls' for its shortcomings, in the same way that Miles accepts the foibles of those around him. It's a pleasant enough thought, but at this length, no prescription for happiness."[31] John Leonard in *New York* magazine valued "a cast that could sail to great and glorious Byzantium," even while conceding that its pace was "a bit too decorous, stately, measured, and slow."[32] Given the complex interaction of persons and town, I can value the film's pacing that allows viewers adequate time for reflection on the mosaic of lives, past and present, which has unfolded before them.

Empire Falls has attracted less critical response than most of Schepisi's films, but as one unpretentious review concluded: "It's a good film, with a great cast, and when you start unravelling what it all means it takes you for a pretty interesting ride."[33] Russo wrote a brilliant novel, and Schepisi made a comparably absorbing cinematic experience.

Chapter Nine

AT HOME AND ABROAD

THE EYE OF THE STORM (2011)

Filming in Australia for the first time since *A Cry in the Dark* twenty-three years earlier, Schepisi found himself again involved in the process of adaptation with *The Eye of the Storm*. Patrick White is not an author who is known for showing too much tenderness towards his characters, and, arguably, in his novel *The Eye of the Storm* (1973) he is at his most misanthropic. In a 2015 interview, Schepisi claimed "What I'm Most Interested in—Always—Is the Humanity of the Piece," a view cited in the title of the article.[1] There must have been some serious challenges, then, for him to come to terms with this particular author.

Adapting White

White won the 1973 Nobel Prize for Literature with *The Eye of the Storm*, but that doesn't mean its nearly 600 pages make for comfortable reading. According to his biographer, David Marr:

> *The Eye of the Storm* was working in White's mind all this time [early 1970s]. There was never a novel he knew so much about before he put it on paper. Even as Ruth [White's mother] lay in Rutland House six years before, he knew he would write about her death, attended by acolytes and besieged by heirs who wished this opulent convalescence would end.... He saw that the core of the novel would be the struggle between himself and that almost senile woman of immense will.[2]

In those sentences, Marr has actually summed up the novel's core, in which Elizabeth Hunter, rich and difficult, is approaching death and is visited by her two children, both of whom have been living overseas and seem to be more concerned with their roles as "heirs" than as devoted offspring. All three are wildly self-preoccupied, though this manifests itself in diverse ways, as are the staff ("acolytes"?) whose function is to do Elizabeth's bidding.

On rereading the novel for the third (and certainly last) time, I was struck by its obsession with physical and psychological ugliness from the very beginning. For instance, Elizabeth is perceived by one of her nurses as "this ruin of an over-indulged and beautiful youth, rustling with fretful spite when not bludgeoning with a brutality only old age is ingenious enough to use."[3] But this is almost benign compared with the fetishistic emphasis on matters such as Elizabeth's "freckly eyelids" (p. 12), or her daughter Dorothy's "horse-faced version" (p. 50) of her mother, or lawyer Wyburn who, observing his wife, is "repelled in particular by that single pockmark on one cheek beside the nose" (p. 274). The novel is strewn with such misanthropic details, and with loving attention to bodily processes such as breaking wind, vomiting, and bed-wetting, often to no discernible purpose. Drawing attention to such persistent, unattractive minutiae is to suggest how far White's attitudes seem at odds with Schepisi's stated intention above: indeed, in this novel, White seems to have a serious distaste for "humanity."

Unsurprisingly perhaps, White's works have not attracted much film attention. There have been several TV versions of his plays; Jim Sharman made a moderately interesting film of the short story, *The Night the Prowler* (1978), for which White wrote his own screenplay; and there was talk, in the early '80s, of a film version of *Voss*, to be directed by Joseph Losey from a screenplay by David Mercer, but that project never came to anything. Schepisi, in the most recent White-inspired venture, filmed *The Eye of the Storm* from a screenplay by former actor Judy Morris, and, characteristically without undue adherence to the original, honed persuasive drama from the family tensions at its heart. Schepisi said of his reading of White's novels that "sometimes I struggled with him" but he admitted to developing "a new-found admiration for his writing"[4] when he approached the matter of adaptation. This did not mean that it would be an easy project to set up, and it took nearly ten years to get the financing ready. Getting some stellar names in place no doubt helped the film's chances.

A Schepisi Film

As will become clear, Schepisi, while largely adhering to the overall narrative arc, which leads of course to Elizabeth's death, has exercised his characteristically fluent shifts among times and places. In this matter, he starts and ends the film with what seem exhilarating shots of the young Elizabeth (Charlotte Rampling) on the beach and along the way there will be such moments from the past. Whereas White's more linear approach nevertheless involves extended passages of recollection, the film will render these with that lithe confluence of past and present, of this place and that, so commonly found in Schepisi's films. One writer in conversation with Schepisi at the time of the film's release noted: "The initial challenge raised in adapting the book was overcoming a static protagonist"[5]—a challenge Schepisi's narrative habits equipped him well to deal with. This makes Sandra Hall's labeling of it as "unashamedly theatrical"[6] rather hard to accept in the light of the narrational maneuvers.

Schepisi has been fortunate in his screenwriters when it comes to adapting works of literary or theatrical origin. Think of John Guare adapting his own play, *Six Degrees of Separation*, or Richard Russo his own novel, *Empire Falls*. Whether it was the original author or Schepisi himself responsible for the screenplay, the director had shown an ongoing interest in the processes of adaptation. As to *The Eye of the Storm*, screenwriter Judy Morris was both an experienced actress and a writer with such admired credentials as *Babe: Pig in the City* (1998), and she has worked the complex relationships in White's nearly 600-page novel into a coherent two-hour film. In the process of rendering these (often-fractious) relationships, a recurring trait in Schepisi's films, she has maintained the tensions without resorting to the obsessive ugliness that so often—and so pointlessly—disfigures the novel.

A further Schepisi trademark is in the way he ensures Ian Baker's camera registers the director's need to reveal faces in relation to the setting. Schepisi claimed that "a viewer needs to be 'inside the picture' all of the time and not noticing the techniques it's using.... The [camera] moves are motivated not only by the characters'" movements so much as by a wish to gain access to them emotionally."[7] In relation to *The Eye of the Storm*, one is constantly aware of the placement of characters in this or that space, such as Elizabeth propped in bed or dressed for the occasion and eased into a chair. In both cases, however, the luxury of her room is part of what governs our knowledge of her inner life as well.

Difficult Lives

The film's narrative is structured around the fact of Elizabeth Hunter's imminent death in her lavish mansion in Centennial Park, Sydney.[8] Biographer Marr writes: "White saw an intimate connection between love and disease, a link he explored most deeply in *The Eye of the Storm*."[9] Marr also noted: "The end for Elizabeth Hunter was the death he feared he had wished on Ruth [his mother]."[10] Such insights may help to account for the novel's preoccupation with the least attractive aspects of his protagonists and for its often-anguished tone. My point is that, without succumbing to the novel's tonal determination to find the worst in everyone, Morris's screenplay essentially retains its overall structure.

As Elizabeth lies on what will be her deathbed, her two children, both of whom have been living overseas, are due to return, as in the novel more interested in ensuring their inheritances than motivated by filial affection. Defective in character in different ways, they have both left scarcely satisfying lives behind them in Europe. All three— mother, son, and daughter—will be seen repairing the ravages to their aging bodies prior to their imminent re-meeting.

Daughter Dorothy (Judy Davis) arrives first. Divorced from her aristocratic French husband, who, not surprisingly given Dorothy's unendearing manner, has found interests elsewhere, she has little to show for her years away but her title: Princess de Lascabanes. Her reunion with her mother, at the latter's lavish home, is a strained affair. Elizabeth, now wigged and made up (the result of very skilled crew members, Cheryl Williams and Kristen Veysey), greets her by saying,

"You're late," and tries to reject Dorothy's kiss. A wide shot of the two of them stresses the separateness of these women.

Son Basil, now *Sir* Basil (Geoffrey Rush), has enjoyed some acting success on the English stage, but his reputation has been somewhat on the wane in recent years, and his two marriages are failed. If Dorothy's manner suggests inner tension, Basil's reflects almost total narcissism and vanity: if he has an inner life, the viewer can only guess at what it might be, as he seems wholly "surface." Before he goes to visit his mother, he is seen first being (in his own view) the life of the party as he sits with a group of admirers (or are they really so?) at a bar. When he finally enters Elizabeth's bedroom, everything about his responses seems acted rather than real, especially in his query: "How is poor old Dorothy?"

The return of the offspring will set the rest of the plot in motion, but it is also important to note at this early stage of the film that there is another group of characters whose attitudes and behavior impinge on Elizabeth's situation. The film reduces the number of her in-house "carers" from five to three: the nurse Flora (Alexandra Schepisi, the director's daughter), who tends to her physical needs and is later not above responding to Basil's sexual overtures; the nurse Mary de Santis (Maria Theodorakis), whose response to her functions seems professionally sound rather than governed by any sense of affection for her bedridden charge; and the housekeeper Lotte Lippmann (Helen Morse), a German refugee of the Holocaust. The last-named has the most intricate relationship with her employer. Helen Morse accounted for this by suggesting that the two women were of the same generation, both were women of the world, and that Lotte "brings some welcome European sensibility and some theatricality to Mrs. Hunter's confined life."[11] When Lotte finally commits suicide, after Mrs. Hunter's death, it was, in Morse's view, "the only time in her on-the-road life when she's ever had a sense of family"[12] and this has now come to an end.

Apart from these three female staff members, a male character, Arnold Wyburn (John Gaden), has an important function in Elizabeth's life and in the film's narrative maneuvers. He serves as her lawyer, meaning that he will be importantly involved in matters to do with her will, but he has also had a more personal connection with her in the past. When it transpires that Basil and Dorothy are planning to move their mother into an aged-care village, Wyburn's wife, Lal (Robyn Nevin), passes this information to Elizabeth, thus interfering with the lawyer's confidentiality in his dealings with Elizabeth's heirs—and leading to his furious outburst against Lal.

The characters referred to above are largely responsible for the film's main action, though in rendering a 589-page novel in two hours of screen time, there are inevitably others who make their presence felt in minor roles. The film is demanding of its actors in the sense that, in its large cast, those in such roles are not always given the screen time to make much impression. However, roles played by the likes of Colin Friels, as a sleazy politician, or Peter Houghton and Trudy Hellier, as the couple who live on what was the Hunters' country house, are just sharply enough delineated in Morris's script to fix their purpose in the film's complex structure, which involves much temporal and spatial darting about.

In structural terms, the film opts for opening on the young Elizabeth caught in a storm on a tropical beach before cutting to the old woman lying in her luxurious bedroom. The film ends on what is virtually a reprise of the opening. In between, there are some crucial occasions when the film returns to the past, largely to dramatize Elizabeth's slippery grasp of the present or, in Dorothy's case, a crucial moment when she recalls her mother's encouraging the sexual advances of her daughter's—Dorothy's—boyfriend. Unlike the more linear approach used in the novel, with its quite long passages of reflection on past events, the film deals with these in fleeting imagistic shifts. As one reviewer wrote: "The director, Fred Schepisi, shows us the history in short glimpses. Brief, almost subliminal scenes, cut and shuffled like a deck of cards."[13]

One curious aspect of the adaptation is that the character of Basil is privileged in the sense of having sole access to voice-over narration. This seems disconcerting, not because it gives him a narrational presence he doesn't have in the novel, but because it seems to imply his thoughts have greater importance than those of either Dorothy or Elizabeth. Nothing else in the film would support such a distinction, so that one can only guess that this is intended to imply the superior star power of Geoffrey Rush. From the outset, it feels like a stylistic miscalculation, at odds with the visual parity accorded both Rush and Davis, as they engage in their various affectations and self-delusions.

While on the subject of how the film goes about dealing with its precursor text, it is worth noting a couple of ways in which Schepisi and the screenplay have trimmed this overlong novel. One very simple economy is in the deletion of Sister Badgery, the least carefully detailed character among the three nurses. She exists as a presence in the novel merely by scattered references to her middle-class snobberies and her late tea-planter husband, and the film doesn't need her. The other departure, again perhaps in the interests of focusing attention during the film's two hours, is that it retains visual inserts of only the past of Elizabeth, not that of Basil or Dorothy. Film, by virtue of its intense visual mimesis, instructs us about how characters look and dress and conduct themselves, in the process obviating the need for filling in a lot of "background." In this case, Dorothy's disappointment is caught in the lineaments of Davis's taut gaze and too-careful couture, while the second-rate "success" of Basil announces itself in Rush's too-loud bonhomie, to say nothing of his yachting jacket and cravat.

And very noticeably, the film avoids that final business of the novel in which the emblematically named nurse, Mary De Santis, commits herself to a new patient, and the next morning, finds her arms "rounded by increasing light" as she sees to the feeding of birds in the garden.[14] This bit of unpersuasive uplift is replaced in the film's last moments by the image I mentioned before, of Elizabeth Hunter's one moment of spontaneous joy on the island beach, where she had weathered "the eye of the storm" and presumably experienced something approaching a state of enlightenment.

Aftertaste

What the film offers is a compelling study of greed, vanity, self-interest, and other assorted moral slipshoddiness. So, it might be said, does the novel, but at least in the film the mere fact of having to embody these characteristics in actual living figures (or their two-dimensional representations) endows them with a humanity that is seldom evident on the page. The characters may be selfish and egoistic, but small moments of other manifestations will keep seeping through, endowing them with vestiges of life that escape their public facades. Without ever descending to sentimentality, Schepisi and his skilled collaborators have achieved a major success in recycling a novel of misanthropic malice and irritatingly over-ornate and affected stylistic posturing by keeping a more humane eye on the lives of the protagonists.

The film is very strongly cast. With Rampling, Rush, and Davis at their commanding best, and with other roles taken by the likes of Helen Morse (in a vivid rendering of the flamboyant Lotte), Colin Friels (politician Athol Shreve), John Gaden (Wyburd), and Robyn Nevin (Lal), the film gets off to a good start. These actors are representative of several decades of Australian cinema, and several of them, like Schepisi, are among the notable pioneers of the 1970s revival. Nevin, indeed, had worked with Schepisi in both *The Priest* and *The Chant of Jimmie Blacksmith*.

Among others who make major contributions to the film is Schepisi's regular cinematographer Ian Baker, who said of the director: "What I like most about Fred is that he's incredibly visual, whereas a lot of directors either don't care or understand about all those other things apart from their actors."[15] This concern for the visual is memorably employed in *The Eye of the Storm*, whether in exterior shots such as the opening and closing beach scenes or in accounting for relationships between characters by the varied ways in which they are placed, whether in Elizabeth's luxurious bedroom and sitting room or in the sprawling country homestead in which the Hunter children grew up and to which they return. In this matter, Melinda Doring's production design discriminates aptly, adding to our grasp of characters through how they are placed in settings, and others such as editor Kate Williams and music director, Paul Grabowsky, who worked on all of Schepisi's films since the turn of the century, help to define the film's tone. Grabowsky was responsible for setting to music the songs Lotte performs for Mrs. Hunter: the lullaby, from a German poem of World War I; and the cabaret act to the tune of "Tingeltangel,"[16] in full costume, the latter the work of Terry Ryan.[17] All of these reinforce the film's insights into the lives concerned.

The point of drawing specific attention to these contributors is to emphasize the film's achievement in taking on a deeply unattractive novel and making something absorbing from it. Whereas almost every page of the novel is pleased to dwell on such details as dandruff, feces, earwax, or wrinkled skin—details that tell us less about the characters than about the author—the film has made the interaction of difficult lives into a largely absorbing experience. As one Australian reviewer said, "Almost all the characters are highly flawed and disagreeable, perhaps reflecting White's misanthropy," adding, "It's an intelligent, well-crafted and, at times, moving and waspishly funny movie."[18] The *Hollywood Reporter* arrived at not-dissimilar views, praising the way "Schepisi corrals a collection of top-shelf talent for *The Eye of the Storm*, an intelligent, visually sumptuous drama . . . that largely manages to transcend its disagreeable subject matter."[19] The film was generally well-received critically, even if *Village Voice* found it to be an "emotionally and psychologically textured melodrama [that] suffers under the weight of its source material," before going on to praise Schepisi's direction for its "measured stateliness, that, in conjunction with Kate Williams's graceful editing, lends quiet intensity to the tumultuous proceedings, at least until a sluggish third act."[20]

Schepisi had plenty of experience in directing films adapted from literary sources that were often demanding in their structure. In some ways, *The Eye of the Storm* may have been the most challenging, not only in dealing with a complex narrative that moves between periods and places but also in coming to terms with White's daunting approach to the "humanity" that was central to Schepisi. Forty years after his first Australian feature, a Schepisi film still exhibits some of the traits that made him a recognizable craftsman and artist.

WORDS AND PICTURES (2013)

At the time of writing, Schepisi's last film stands as *Words and Pictures*, which, like *Roxanne*, was filmed in Canada and shares with the earlier film some generic characteristics. However, it seems not to have been nearly so commercially successful, and in an interview with Schepisi included on the DVD for the film, he perhaps hints at why this is so. When the interviewer asked him: "Would you say it's a super-intellectual romantic comedy?" Schepisi replied: "I would, but no one would go to see it!"[21]

The Title

The rather prosaic title hardly suggests the expectations that audiences may usually have of the romantic comedy genre, and in fact the film is much more obviously concerned with ideas than is commonly associated with that genre. However, as one reviewer pointed out: "One of the film's strengths is what it is not: the didactic discussion of art and ideas it could have been."[22] There is indeed plenty of dialogue, but the film bears witness to Schepisi's own comment on this matter: "I think you should shoot dialogue as action . . . And dialogue isn't necessarily just being on the person talking."[23]

In fact, it has strong claims to be considered one of the director's sharpest films, and one that has deserved much more notice than seems to have been the case. At the box office, it appears to have grossed a little over $3 million compared with *Roxanne*'s $40 million;[24] it was apparently never shown in the UK,[25] and had only fleeting release in Australia. I shall argue that, if this is to be Schepisi's last film, he has finished on a high note: the film warrants serious reconsideration. In his own view on the film's unduly limited success, he reflected:

> There was a small but reasonable amount of money for its release in America, but the distributors insisted on selling it as a romantic comedy, and it was way more than that. People going to see it on that basis will be dissatisfied in the first ten minutes when it seems to be about literature and art, whereas, if you go along knowing you're going to see a more complex film about kids and teaching, etc., then you're in for a more interesting experience.[26]

Words and Pictures had a nearly four-year struggle to get made. In the same DVD interview, Schepisi recounted how "exceptionally difficult it was for a picture with any depth of intelligence to get going" and how finally there was "a group of investors from Texas who wanted to see the film made."[27] There may be an element of cynicism in his dismissal of so much contemporary filmmaking as "popcorn cinema," and therefore at odds with the likes of *Words and Pictures*, but given the reflective tone of the resulting film, it is not too hard to accept the idea of its attracting more discerning audiences than those drawn to "popcorn cinema."

Given that some of Schepisi's most notable films were adapted from novels and plays—that is, from texts dependent on words into a medium in which images, or "pictures," are at least as important as words—the title of this most recent film could almost work as a title for his autobiography, if he ever chooses to write one. In films such as *Plenty, A Cry in the Dark, Six Degrees of Separation*, and *Last Orders*, all derived from "words," much of their holding power derives from his and/or his screenwriters' grasp of the idiomatic individuality of the characters and their ambient communities. Certainly, however, in all of them, vivid "pictures" also command our rapt attention, whether of the Manhattan skyline or of Canterbury Cathedral. The title may not have lured vast audiences, but on several re-viewings of the film, I find that it comes to seem wholly appropriate, and not remotely, as one reviewer claimed, "flat and prosaic."[28]

Lives that Compete and Converge

It is perhaps not unusual in the romantic comedy genre to find lives that compete and converge, but in *Words and Pictures* the parallel between the protagonistic (and antagonistic) couple seems at first so fixed that it is not so easy to anticipate convergence. Jack Marcus (Clive Owen) is writer and an English teacher with a passion for words—and a drinking problem. Dina Delsanto (Juliette Binoche) is an artist and art teacher whose rheumatoid arthritis has inhibited her mobility. What they have in common is that each is a potentially inspirational teacher in a middle-class prep school, she responsible for the Honors Art class, in which she is uncompromising in dealing with students, he for the Honors English class, in which he insists that words are what life is essentially about.

To the accompaniment of Paul Grabowsky's engaging soundtrack, the film opens with alternating images of Jack and Dina. First, she is glimpsed applying lipstick; second, he is seen while getting dressed. Then she steps outside with the aid of her walking stick, while he gathers up his papers, after which they drive off severally. These brief shots induct us into the film's central preoccupation with these two diverse personalities, both of whom "[have] a secret they try mightily to hide from the world."[29]

The film then goes on to establish the two characters in their teaching roles. Jack, who suffers from writer's block as well as alcoholism, talks to his students about John Updike and his prose, and sets them an assignment to write something that creates an image to "shake" him, something he's never thought of before. After the class, the school's principal, Rashid (Navid Negahban), gently chides Jack for always being late, and this, along with Jack's somewhat bedraggled look and slouching deportment, suggest a life that is a bit of a mess. By contrast, Dina in her classroom is austere, telling her students that she "has no curiosity about [their] private lives"; that is not what art is about, and she is making no attempt to woo them.

Gerald Di Pego's screenplay is carefully, but without undue schematism, preparing us for a contrasting pair with serious limitations and yet with a capacity to strike sparks from each other. As Clive Owen said: "We were helped by a really great script. We're at loggerheads with each other, but there *was* attraction," while Juliette Binoche's view of the pair was as follows: "There's a huge need that's not fulfilled yet . . . [and] the connection comes from that need."[30] Until this need is recognized, let alone fulfilled, there is comedy in the strained discourse between them (and their one sexual encounter certainly does not initiate bliss). He is incessantly engaging other staff members with word games, and when he asks for a five-syllable reply, she offers: "Blah blah blah blah blah." She tells a friend: "That English teacher is a madman."

Shortly after at their homes, Jack is seen failing to get on with his writing while a frustrated Dina slashes her painting. Back in class, Jack claims that "words make things better, not pictures," while she insists that "a picture is worth a thousand words," a statement he will reverse when, as a student tells her, "Mr. Marcus has declared war on you." This declaration is announced on a poster: "Words are worth a thousand pictures." To this, her reply is: "A picture is worth a thousand lies." Such quotations may suggest that the screenplay is spelling out its eponymous concerns too explicitly, but the lively talk about art and words raises the film to a level of intelligence different from the conventional "sparring" of romantic comedy leads. Also, the talk about these is incarnated in the emerging and engaging reality of the pair who expound them, revealing their weaknesses as well as their obsessions in the process. Jack is seen drunkenly smashing things in his study, while Dina's physical debility hampers her painting, despite the harness equipment meant to help her as she tries to paint on the floor. (In passing, it may be mentioned that Binoche, herself a visual artist of real talent, apparently created all of Dina's artworks. Perhaps this helps to account for the seeming authenticity of the art she makes.)

Two "events" work towards an ending that seems seriously gratifying instead of merely inevitable. First, there is the matter of the school's magazine in which Dina, against Jack's wishes, insists that pictures should be included. The other is the "Words and Pictures" school occasion in which both Jack and Dina take the microphone to make the cases for their respective media. Naturally both are celebrated as central to "mak[ing] us feel our best," but, lest this should sound as if the film is settling too easily for a "feel-good" ending, there is a less charming exchange outside the hall. "You ice-cold bitch" is Jack's sweet overture, which Dina counters with: "You drunken art-wrecking bastard." Then they both giggle and finally embrace. If the latter may suggest an oversimplification of what has been a complex film, the exchange and giggle prior to the embrace seems to imply that, though they may now be on kissing terms, they haven't forgotten what has made them sparring partners throughout the film.

How the Words and Pictures Get Together

The two most obvious collaborators in this venture are of course the stars, Clive Owen and Juliette Binoche. Both have had long and distinguished careers, often in art-house fare but equally adeptly in more broadly popular films. Here, each achieves a tonal exactitude that never falters as they bring this gifted, flawed pair to such persuasive life that the final acknowledgment of a possible future together has been utterly accounted for. Neither plays for easy sympathy, but in their responses to Di Pego's sharp and witty screenplay they contrive to suggest a couple who may yet have individual quirks to indulge even as they commit, at least tentatively, to a future together.

Schepisi has a good record in the romantic comedy genre—think of *Roxanne* or *I.Q.*—but it is at least debatable that in Owen and Binoche he had his subtlest purveyors of the leading couple's give-and-take. As one critic said, "Schepisi elicits strong turns from the two leads, who exhibit moments of palpable chemistry," though he felt that other cast members, playing assorted staff and students at the school, "feel little more than sketches."[31] There may be some truth in that final remark, but this is essentially a film in which the two protagonists and their life-views are what holds the narrative together. There are good moments for Bruce Greenwood as the colleague most disposed to liking Jack, for Christian Schneider as Jack's son, disaffected by his father's unreliable behavior, and for several of the actors cast as students, especially Valerie Tien as Dina's most promising pupil. Admittedly, none of these performers has much to work with, but each contributes to our grasp of the haphazardly developing relationship between Jack and Dina.

If Schepisi's filmography is rife with insightful acting performances, it is also notable for his frequent recurring reliance on other distinguished practitioners, and in *Words and Pictures*, his most recent film to date, several of these were still making notable contributions to its artistic success—even if this was not matched by box-office returns. Above all, there is Ian Baker, who shot all but one of Schepisi's films, but rewatching *Words and Pictures* I can't but disagree with Baker's account of his work on the film. He said:

> I guess the hardest film I've done from the point of view of making it work was *Words and Pictures*, which was all shot in a boring school with low ceilings. You know it's not going to look great because you're in a boring location, and you struggle to do things to make it look different every time you're in one of these classrooms where there was quite a bit of drama going on. You do what you can to make it dramatically interesting.[32]

Baker—working on the production design of another Schepisi veteran, Patrizia von Brandenstein—ensures that the schoolroom, far from being "boring," has a convincing sense of reality. One accepts the ordinary functionality of the spaces—whether of classroom or staff lounge, or of Jack's and Dina's home quarters—as sites for our further insights into the central duo. One critic summed up accurately how Baker's "crisp images showcase the authentic production design of von Brandenstein and the verdant surroundings."[33]

Editor Peter Honess is another longtime associate of the director, and these three account for much of the film's distinctive look. Schepisi's films are in general less reliant on such standard Hollywood procedures as the shot-reverse-shot technique between two players, preferring more often the placement of his key figures in a larger space in order to establish their connections with the place, in which they move around with minimal cutting. This is the case in this most recent film, where it is crucial for us to see his two main characters in relation to environments that contribute to our knowledge of them—and to the final lakeside vista, which offers tentative promise of broader, more benign horizons.

As Schepisi sees it, "*Words and Pictures* . . . is an adult film that isn't just a romantic comedy but rather a "real" story of two people trying to find their way forward as they experience great difficulties in pursuing their deepest passions."[34] A persuasive summation of its achievement. *Words and Pictures* may not be Schepisi's greatest film, but it deserves more considered attention than it has been given—and if it turns out to be his farewell to cinema, it shows some of his recurring qualities in finely sophisticated form.

CONCLUSION

It was probably not uncommon for Australian film directors to set up productions during the revival there in the 1970s, but, as noted earlier, several of them, such as Peter Weir, Bruce Beresford, and Gillian Armstrong, contrived to deal with the problems involved and to go on from their home territory to overseas success. Fred Schepisi is a prime example of this phenomenon, and in this study it has been interesting—and rewarding—to come to terms with his major achievements in three continents. There were often difficulties in getting these productions off the ground and steering them towards completion, and some of these are discussed, but the results, the films themselves, have been my chief concern here.

In whichever continent he was working, Schepisi's films, however consciously, seemed to register the national identity of their site of production and this was often an essential element in their thematic and narrative procedures. It is as if he adapted himself fully to this situation, so that one doesn't feel as if one is faced with a geographical hybrid when viewing such disparate works as, say, *A Cry in the Dark*, *Last Orders*, and *Empire Falls*. Australia clearly mattered to him, and he returned to it regularly, but the films he made elsewhere don't seem to resonate with his country of origin. He became an international filmmaker, achieving success in multiple environments.

In Australia *The Chant of Jimmie Blacksmith* and *A Cry in the Dark*, in the UK *Last Orders*, and in the US *Six Degrees of Separation* and the TV series *Empire Falls* seemed to me, on close exploration, to constitute those "major achievements" referred to above. As a sign of this, they have received more extended treatment than some of his other dozen features. However, many of the others, while perhaps less ambitious in their scope and aspirations, have plenty to offer; in fact, his last film at the time of writing, *Words and Pictures*, is as intelligent and beguiling a romantic comedy as any made in the last decade.

A recent interview draws attention to some of the difficulties referred to above in relation to two films Schepisi has sought to make but which, for assorted reasons, have not taken off. When I asked about whether *Andorra*, announced in 2016, was still a possibility, his reply was:

> It died because we couldn't get the money. We'd assembled a great cast [including Gillian Anderson, Clive Owen, and Vanessa Redgrave] and chosen great locations. Some of the people we were involved with thought we could do it on the money we had, which was mostly government subsidy between Italy and Australia, but we couldn't make the film that was required. It wasn't easy to get that cast together, but fortunately they wanted to work with me. They hung in with me when we had to move, but then Clive had to do another picture, which was presumably confirmed. Once you get a cast like that, there's a lot of jockeying to get the timing right, so that it works for all of them.[1]

Since the collapse of *Andorra*, he co-wrote a film with Judy Morris, who wrote *Eye of the Storm*. It was "a sort of allegory about Australia and China trying to get together, it's an adult love story, set in the wine fields in northern China and Redhill here [Victoria]. It was all signed up and looked as if it was going ahead, when the people in China decided they wanted to make an entirely different film. There were other factors but I'd still like to get it going."[2] Certainly Schepisi has encountered plenty of challenges in the course of his long career, but there have been, as suggested above, a generous share of successes as well. No doubt the acumen he acquired early on in dealing with the industrial and commercial aspects of filmmaking has placed him in good stead, thus enabling him to articulate in cinematic terms his craftsmanship and his essentially humanist approach to his projects in the face of production challenges.

...

Dealing with the films chronologically, I have found this approach equally useful for the way it drew attention to the emergence of thematic and stylistic continuities *and* to Schepisi's adaptability to matters of filmmaking practice in three continents and to the challenges of generic diversity. Writing in 1992 about Schepisi and other Australian filmmakers of the "revival," my coauthor and I characterized their films as falling between art-house and classical Hollywood cinema, as if this were a matter for criticism.[3] In the light of working my way through Schepisi's output, I can only agree with a later critic who wrote: "Schepisi's inability to fit into *either* and yet, in a sense, do *both* should not be regarded as failure."[4] He was not a director to be confined by labels such as these.

As to those "continuities," one of the most striking, especially in the features of the first couple of decades, was his sympathetic preoccupation with the idea of the outsider in relation to a larger community. First was the boy who may or may not have a religious vocation in *The Devil's Playground* and the half-Aboriginal who "declares war" on Federation Australia in *Jimmie Blacksmith*. Then, in the US, were the two protagonists on the run from the film's settlements in *Barbarosa* and the Neanderthal eponym in *Iceman* and the nasally grotesque police officer in *Roxanne*. Most memorable and intriguing of all was the intrusive Will Smith character in *Six Degrees of Separation*. Back in Australia, the legally embattled Chamberlains are pushed into outsider status by a sensationalist media response to their tragic situation in *A Cry in the Dark*, and in the brilliant US series, *Empire Falls*, the decent guy at the center of its narrative is frequently found at odds with the world around him.

Merely listing these instances is not sufficient: they are indicative of a humane approach to what is often a crucially demanding conflict. What is also impressive is that this thematic concern is incarnated in so striking a range of genres. On record as saying that "the Humanity of the Piece" constitutes his prime interest,[5] Schepisi can make the outsider status work for comedy as well as for more serious, even tragic outcomes in other genres, whether Western or science fiction. In stylistic terms, this status is frequently rendered in the placement of the outsider figure at a remove, sometimes vulnerable, sometimes threatening, and this reminds one of another recurring characteristic of Schepisi's work: his potent rendering of the interaction of person and place, in all manner of generic situations.

CONCLUSION

This interaction isn't just a matter of narrative texture, though that, of course, is of central importance. Think of Miles Roby (Ed Harris) and his complex life in the context of the difficulties of the waning town in *Empire Falls* or Sean Connery's author in "glasnostic" Moscow in *The Russia House*. What is also striking, again and again, is the stylistic representation of characters in their physical setting. It is not so much eloquent close-ups one recalls at moments such as in *Six Degrees of Separation*, when the rich Kittredges seem to be so opulently placed as to almost preclude closeness, rendering the intruding young man almost poignantly separate; or in *The Eye of the Storm*, when the lack of real warmth and affection between the aged Elizabeth Hunter (Charlotte Rampling) and her awkward daughter is signified by their distance from each other in the mother's luxurious bedroom.

My point is that, no matter the genre or continent he is working, Schepisi has established recurring patterns of interest and their imagistic renderings. Further, location has always seemed to matter—and he talks about its importance and its challenges—whether it is a matter of establishing the sense of a provincial town, as in *Roxanne*, or the daunting threat of outback Australia in both *Jimmie Blacksmith* and *A Cry in the Dark*. He emerged as a director of ideas as well as one who rendered these in aptly chosen words and pictures, to quote the title of his last film.

If adaptability, whether in relation to filmmaking conditions in different continents or to a range of genres, is a key feature of his career, another recurring aspect has been his readiness to engage with the processes of adaptation. This has often entailed close working relationships with the antecedent authors or playwrights, several of these being major figures in their own media. He has been aware that the filmmaker's function is to make something new in transferring a play or novel to the screen, but, without any sense of reverential fidelity to the original, he has always insisted that it was his function to do "justice" to it.[6] With writers, as well as with other collaborators before and behind the camera, he seems to have been both a director with a clear sense of what he wanted to achieve, and one with an openness to suggestion from those others involved. Perhaps above all it is his long association with cinematographer Ian Baker that helps to account for the visual and emotional texture of his films, though he has also sustained several other working relationships—for example, with production designers and editors—that have made significant contributions to his output.

In a thorough evaluation of Schepisi's achievement, it is important not merely to dwell entirely on such positive matters as his versatility in responding to the challenges of different genres and different production circumstances, impressive though these may be. However, the only quibble that seems to me worth making—and one that I have made in a couple of chapters—is a sometimes meandering approach to structure. In a film such as *It Runs in the Family* there is a tendency to put too many characters and events before us without a sufficiently firm structure to hold them together or to place them tightly in a narrative or thematic arc that would guarantee their coherence.

More often, though, his tonal command and skill in maneuvering between various times and places ensure that coherence, as in such masterworks as *Six Degrees of Separation*, *Last Orders*, and *Empire Falls*. In such films, Schepisi can persuade us that we may fully understand the present if we are fully informed about the ways the past has borne on the lives at issue—and to imply how their interaction may shape their future. His concern for the wholeness of these lives, and the influences that have made them as they are, confirm the sensibility of a major filmmaker—a humanist craftsman and an artist.

FILMOGRAPHY

INDUSTRIAL DOCUMENTARIES (INCOMPLETE)

The Shape of Quality 1965, 27 minutes
Director: Fred Schepisi
Writer: Fred Schepisi
Photography: Howard Rubie
Editor: Brian Kavanagh
Music: Bruce Clarke and Frank Smith
Narrator: John Royle
Cinesound Production

People Make Papers 1965, 26 minutes
Director: Fred Schepisi
Writer: Fred Schepisi
Photography: Peter Purvis
Editor: Brian Kavanagh
Cinesound Production

A Hundred-Odd Years from Now 1968, 17 minutes
Director: Fred Schepisi
Writers: Weatherhead & Stitt
Photography: Lars Goodlach
Editor: Michael O'Donnell
Music: Frank Smith
Design: Weatherhead & Stitt
Cast: Ian Bremner, Lew Walker, Will Timmerman, Susy Kendall
The Film House

The Plus Factor 1970, 12 minutes
Director: Fred Schepisi
Writers: Fred Schepisi
Photography: Volk Mol
Editor: Brian Kavanagh
Music: Bruce Clarke
Design: Weatherhead & Stitt
The Film House

Onward Speed 1971, 14 minutes
Director: Fred Schepisi
Writer: Fred Schepisi
Photography: Ian Baker
Editor: Gail Norton
Cast: Rhonda Finlayson, Jon Finlayson
The Film House

Tomorrow's Canberra 1972, 34 minutes
Director: Fred Schepisi
Writers: Fred Schepisi
Photography: Ian Baker
Editor: K. Michael Reed
Music: Bruce Smeaton
The Film House for the Australian Commonwealth Film Unit

SHORTS

Party 1970, 20 minutes
Director: Fred Schepisi
Screenplay: Russell Beedles
Production Facilities and Technical Crew: Staff and Students, Swinburne College of Technology Film and Television Department
Cast: Jon Finlayson (Norman), Di O'Connor (Vera), John Hanson (Frank), Marion Edley (landlady), Martin Phelan (Felix)
The Film House

Can't You Hear Me Callin', Caroline 1971
Director: Fred Schepisi
Screenplay: Fred Schepisi
Production Facilities and Technical Crew: Staff and Students, Swinburne College of Technology Film and Television Department
Entertainment Media

The Priest 1973, 27 minutes
(Part 3 of ***Libido***, a four-part feature)
Director: Fred Schepisi
Writers: Thomas Keneally
Photography: Ian Baker
Editor: Brian Kavanagh
Music: Bruce Smeaton
Cast: Arthur Dignam (Father Burn), Robyn Nevin (Sister Caroline), Vivean Gray (elderly nun)
Producers and Directors Guild of Australia

FEATURES

The Devil's Playground 1976, 107 minutes
Producer: Fred Schepisi
Director: Fred Schepisi
Screenplay: Fred Schepisi
Photography: Ian Baker
Editor: Brian Kavanagh
Music: Bruce Smeaton
Production Design: Trevor Ling
Cast: Arthur Dignam (Brother Francine), Simon Burke (Tom Allen), Nick Tate (Brother Victor), Charles McCallum (Brother Sebastian), John Frawley (Brother Celian), Jonathan Hardy (Brother Arnold), Thomas Keneally (Father Marshall), Jon Diedrich (Fitz), Sheila Florance (Mrs. Sullivan)
The Film House

The Chant of Jimmie Blacksmith 1978, 108 minutes
Producer: Fred Schepisi
Director: Fred Schepisi
Screenplay: Fred Schepisi (based on the novel by Thomas Keneally)
Photography: Ian Baker
Editor: Brian Kavanagh
Music: Bruce Smeaton
Production Design: Wendy Dickson
Cast: Tommy Lewis (Jimmie Blacksmith), Freddy Reynolds (Mort Blacksmith), Ray Barrett (Farrell), Jack Thompson (Rev. Neville), Angela Punch (Gilda Marshall), Steve Dodd (Tabidgi), Peter Carroll (McCready), Robyn Nevin (Mrs. McCready), Ruth Cracknell (Mrs. Newby), Don Crosby (Jack Newby), Elizabeth Alexander (Petra Graff).
The Film House

Barbarosa 1982, 90 minutes
Producer: Paul N. Lazarus III
Director: Fred Schepisi
Screenplay: William D. Wittliff
Photography: Ian Baker
Editor: Don Zimmerman and David Ramirez
Music: Bruce Smeaton
Production Design Consultant: Leon Ericksen
Cast: Willie Nelson (Barbarosa), Gary Busey (Karl Westover), Isela Vega (Josephina), Gilbert Roland (Don Braulio), Danny De La Paz (Eduardo), Alma Martinez (Juanita), Howland Chamberlain (Emil), George Voskovec (Herman)
Universal

Iceman 1984, 100 minutes
Producers: Patrick Palmer and Norman Jewison
Director: Fred Schepisi
Screenplay: Chris Proser and John Drimmer
Photography: Ian Baker
Editor: Billy Weber (and Don Zimmerman [uncredited])
Music: Bruce Smeaton

Makeup Creator: Michael Westmore
Cast: Timothy Hutton (Dr. Stanley Shephard), Lindsay Crouse (Dr. Diane Brady), John Lone (Charlie), Josef Sommer (Whitman), David Strathairn (Dr. Singe), Danny Glover (Loomis)
Universal

Plenty 1985, 121 minutes
Producers: Edward R. Pressman and Joseph Papp
Director: Fred Schepisi
Screenplay: David Hare (based on his play)
Photography: Ian Baker
Editor: Peter Honess
Music: Bruce Smeaton
Production Design: Richard Macdonald
Cast: Meryl Streep (Susan Traherne), Charles Dance (Raymond Brock), Tracey Ullman (Alice Park), Sam Neill (Lazar), John Gielgud (Sir Leonard Darwin), Sting (Mick), Ian McKellen (Sir Andrew Charleson)
Pressman Productions, RKO Pictures

Roxanne 1987, 103 minutes
Producers: Michael Rachmil and Daniel Melnick
Director: Fred Schepisi
Screenplay: Steve Martin (based on the play *Cyrano de Bergerac* by Edmond Rostand)
Photography: Ian Baker
Editor: John Scott
Music: Bruce Smeaton
Production Design: Jack De Govia
Cast: Steve Martin (C. D. Bales), Daryl Hannah (Roxanne Kowalski), Rick Rossovich (Chris McConnell), Shelley Duvall (Dixie), John Kapelos (Chuck), Fred Willard (Mayor), Michael J. Pollard (Andy)
Columbia

A Cry in the Dark/Evil Angels 1988, 120 minutes
Producers: Menahem Golan, Yoram Globus, and Verity Lambert
Director: Fred Schepisi

Screenplay: Robert Caswell and Fred Schepisi (based on the book by John Bryson)
Photography: Ian Baker
Editor: Jill Bilcock
Music: Bruce Smeaton
Production Design: Wendy Dickson and George Liddle
Cast: Meryl Streep (Lindy Chamberlain), Sam Neill (Michael Chamberlain), Bruce Myles (Ian Barker), Neil Fitzpatrick (John Phillips), Charles Tingwell (Justice James Muirhead), Maurie Fields (Justice Dennis Barritt), Nick Tate (Graeme Charlwood), Lewis Fitz-Gerald (Stuart Tipple)
Warner Bros.

The Russia House 1990, 123 minutes
Producers: Paul Maslansky and Fred Schepisi
Director: Fred Schepisi
Screenplay: Tom Stoppard (based on novel by John le Carré)
Photography: Ian Baker
Editor: Peter Honess (and Beth Jochem Besterveld [uncredited])
Music: Jerry Goldsmith
Production Design: Richard Macdonald
Cast: Sean Connery (Barley), Michelle Pfeiffer (Katya), James Fox (Ned), Michael Kitchen (Clive), Roy Scheider (Russell), John Mahoney (Brady), J. T. Walsh (Quinn), Ken Russell (Walter), Klaus Maria Brandauer (Dante/Yakov)
Metro-Goldwyn-Mayer/Pathé Entertainment

Mr. Baseball 1992, 108 minutes
Producers: Fred Schepisi, Doug Claybourne, and Robert Newmeyer
Director: Fred Schepisi
Screenplay: Gary Ross, Kevin Wade, and Monte Merrick (from the story by Theo Pelletier and John Junkerman)
Photography: Ian Baker
Editor: Peter Honess (and Beth Jochem Besterveld [uncredited])
Music: Jerry Goldsmith
Production Design: Ted Howarth

Cast: Tom Selleck (Jack Elliot), Ken Takakura (Uchiyama), Aya Takanashi (Hiroko Uchiyama), Dennis Haysbert (Max "Hammer" Dubois), Toshi Shioya (Yoji Nishimura)
Universal

Six Degrees of Separation 1993, 112 minutes
Producers: Fred Schepisi and Arnon Milchan
Director: Fred Schepisi
Screenplay: John Guare (based on his play)
Photography: Ian Baker
Editor: Peter Honess
Music: Jerry Goldsmith
Production Design: Patrizia von Brandenstein
Cast: Stockard Channing (Ouisa), Will Smith (Paul), Donald Sutherland (Flan), Ian McKellen (Geoffrey), Mary Beth Hurt (Kitty), Bruce Davison (Larkin), Richard Masur (Dr. Fine), Heather Graham (Elizabeth), J. J. Abrams (Doug), Kitty Carlisle Hart (Mrs. Bannister)
Metro-Goldwyn-Mayer

I.Q. 1994, 95 minutes
Producers: Carol Baum and Fred Schepisi
Director: Fred Schepisi
Screenplay: Andy Breckman and Michael Leeson
Photography: Ian Baker
Editor: Jill Bilcock
Music: Jerry Goldsmith
Production Design: Stuart Wurtzel
Cast: Tim Robbins (Ed Walters), Meg Ryan (Catherine Boyd), Walter Matthau (Albert Einstein), Lou Jacobi (Kurt Godel), Gene Saks (Boris Podolsky), Joseph Maher (Nathan Liebknecht), Stephen Fry (James Moreland).
Paramount

Fierce Creatures 1997, 95 minutes
Producers: Michael Shamberg and John Cleese
Directors: Robert Young and Fred Schepisi

Screenplay: John Cleese and Iain Johnson (and William Goldman [uncredited])
Photography: Adrian Biddle and Ian Baker
Editor: Robert Gibson
Music: Jerry Goldsmith
Production Design: Roger Murray-Leach
Cast: John Cleese (Rollo Lee), Jamie Lee Curtis (Willa Weston), Kevin Kline (Rod McCain/Vince McCain), Michael Palin (Adrian "Bugsy" Malone), Ronnie Corbett (Reggie Sea Lions), Bille Brown (Neville Coltrane), Carey Lowell (Cub Felines), Robert Lindsay (Sydney Lotterby)
Universal

Last Orders 2001, 109 minutes
Producers: Elisabeth Robinson and Fred Schepisi
Directors: Fred Schepisi
Screenplay: Fred Schepisi (based on the novel by Graham Swift)
Photography: Brian Tufano
Editor: Kate Williams
Music: Paul Grabowsky
Production Design: Tim Harvey
Cast: Michael Caine (Jack), Tom Courtenay (Vic), David Hemmings (Lenny), Bob Hoskins (Ray), Helen Mirren (Amy), Ray Winstone (Vince), J. J. Field (Young Jack), Cameron Fitch (Young Vic), Nolan Hemmings (Young Lenny), Anatol Yusef (Young Ray), Stephen McCole (Young Vince), Kelly Reilly (Young Amy), George Innes (Bernie), Laura Morelli (June)
Sony Pictures Classics

It Runs in the Family 2003, 109 minutes
Producer: Michael Douglas
Director: Fred Schepisi
Screenplay: Jesse Wigutow
Photography: Ian Baker
Editor: Kate Williams
Music: Paul Grabowsky
Production Design: Patrizia von Brandenstein

Cast: Michael Douglas (Alex Gromberg), Kirk Douglas (Mitchell Gromberg), Rory Culkin (Eli Gromberg), Cameron Douglas (Asher Gromberg), Diana Douglas (Evelyn Gromberg), Michelle Monaghan (Peg Maloney), Sarita Choudhury (Suzie), Bernadette Peters (Rebecca Gromberg), Mark Hammer (Stephen Gromberg), Irene Gorovaia (Abby Staley)
Metro-Goldwyn-Mayer Studios, Furthur Films

Empire Falls (TV movie) 2005, 188 minutes
Producer: William Teitler
Director: Fred Schepisi
Screenplay: Richard Russo (based on his novel)
Photography: Ian Baker
Editor: Kate Williams
Music: Paul Grabowsky
Production Design: Stuart Wurtzel
Cast: Ed Harris (Miles Roby), Philip Seymour Hoffman (Charlie Mayne), Helen Hunt (Janine Roby), Paul Newman (Max Roby), Robin Wright Penn (Grace Roby), Aidan Quinn (David Roby), Joanne Woodward (Francine Roby), Dennis Farina (Walt Comeau), Danielle Panabaker (Tick Roby), Theresa Russell (Charlene), William Fichtner (Jimmy Minty), Estelle Parsons (Bea), Kate Burton (Cindy Whiting)
HBO Films

The Eye of the Storm 2011, 114 minutes
Producers: Gregory J. Read and Antony Waddington
Director: Fred Schepisi
Screenplay: Judy Morris (based on the novel by Patrick White)
Photography: Ian Baker
Editor: Kate Williams
Music: Paul Grabowsky
Production Design: Melinda Doring
Cast: Charlotte Rampling (Elizabeth Hunter), Geoffrey Rush (Basil Hunter), Judy Davis (Dorothy de Lascabanes), Helen Morse (Lotte), Alexandra Schepisi (Flora), John Gaden (Arnold Wyburd), Robyn Nevin (Lal)
Paper Bark Films Pty Ltd.

Words and Pictures 2013, 111 minutes
Producer: Curtis Burch and Fred Schepisi
Director: Fred Schepisi
Screenplay: Gerald Di Pego
Photography: Ian Baker
Editor: Peter Honess
Music: Paul Grabowsky
Production Design: Patrizia von Brandenstein
Cast: Clive Owen (Jack Marcus), Juliette Binoche (Dina Delsanto), Bruce Davison (Walt), Navid Negahban (Rashid), Amy Brennerman (Elspeth), Valerie Tian (Emily), Adam DiMarco (Swint)
Latitude Productions, Lascaux Films

NOTES

PREFACE

1. Author interview with Schepisi, September 2018.

CHAPTER ONE: EARLY DAYS

1. For details of Schepisi's early life, see Tom Ryan, ed., *Fred Schepisi: Interviews* (Jackson: University Press of Mississippi, 2017), xx–xxi.
2. Author interview with Schepisi, November 2014.
3. Sue Matthews, *35mm Dreams: Conversations with Five Directors* (Ringwood, Victoria: Penguin Books, 1984), 12.
4. Author interview with Schepisi, August 2018.
5. Matthews, 24.
6. Author interview with Schepisi, August 2018.
7. Author interview with Schepisi, August 2018.
8. Author interview with Schepisi, August 2018.
9. In interview with Tom Ryan, 2015, in Ryan, ed., 155.
10. Ryan, ed., xxiv.

CHAPTER TWO: EMERGING FILMMAKER

1. John B. Murray, "The Guild—A Brief History," essay accompanying the DVD released by Guild Productions Pty Ltd. (n.d.).
2. Tom Ryan, ed., *Fred Schepisi: Interviews* (Jackson: University Press of Mississippi, 2017), xiii.
3. Andrew Pike and Ross Cooper, *Australian Film, 1900–1977* (Melbourne: Oxford University Press, revised edition, 1998), 270.
4. Author interview with Keneally, January 2020.

5. Meaghan Morris, "Personal Relationships and Sexuality," in Scott Murray, ed., *New Australian Cinema* (Melbourne: Thomas Nelson, 1980), 133.

6. Scott Murray, *Australian Cinema* (St. Leonard's, NSW: Allen & Unwin, with Australian Film Commission, 1994), 76.

7. Graham Shirley and Brian Adams, *Australian Cinema: The First Eighty Years* (Australia: Angus & Robertson Publishers and Currency Press, 1983), 267.

8. "Ocker" was a term used in the 1960s to refer to a rough, uncultivated Australian male.

9. Tom O'Regan, "The Ocker Films," in Albert Moran and Tom O'Regan, eds., *The Australian Screen* (Ringwood, Victoria: Penguin Books, 1989), 83.

10. John B. Murray.

11. Special feature on DVD of *Libido*.

12. Author interview with Keneally, January 17, 2020.

13. Author interview with Keneally, January 17, 2020.

14. Interview in Sue Mathews, *35mm Dreams: Five Directors* (Ringwood, Victoria: Penguin Books, 1984), 35.

15. Morris, in Murray, ed., 140.

16. Morris, in Murray, ed., 140.

17. Pike and Cooper, 270.

18. Figures quoted in Susan Dermody and Elizabeth Jacka, *The Screening of Australia: Volume 1* (Sydney: Currency Press, 1987), 169.

19. *Nation Review*, 13–19 (April 1973) (Thomas) and 19–29 (April 1973) (Ellis).

20. Sandra Hall, review originally appeared in the *Bulletin*, later anthologized in Adelaide et al., *Critical Business: The New Australian Cinema in Review* (Rigby, 1985), 13.

21. Susan Dermody and Elizabeth Jacka, *The Screening of Australia: Volume 1* (Sydney: Currency Press, 1988), 163.

22. Author interview with Schepisi, Melbourne, December 4, 2014.

23. Susan Dermody and Elizabeth Jacka, *The Screening of Australia: Anatomy of a National Cinema, Volume 2* (Sydney: Currency Press, 1988), 110.

24. Tom O'Regan, *Australian National Cinema* (London and New York: Routledge, 1996), 197.

25. In Sue Matthews, *35mm Dreams*, 36

26. Author interview with Schepisi, Melbourne, December 4, 2014.

27. Author interview with Schepisi, Melbourne, December 4, 2014.

28. Neil Rattigan, *Images of Australia* (Dallas: Southern Methodist University Press, 1991), 109–10.

29. Peter Malone, "Revisiting *The Devil's Playground*," in Malone, ed., *Through a Catholic Lens: Religious Perspectives of Nineteen Film Directors from Around the World* (Lanham, MD: Rowman & Littlefield, 2007), 33.

30. Rattigan, 109,
31. In Matthews, 36.
32. Author interview with Schepisi, Melbourne, December 4, 2014.
33. Pauline Kael, "The Devil in the Flesh," *New Yorker*, December 7, 1981.
34. *A Portrait of the Artist as a Young Man* was published in 1922. The 1977 film was directed by Joseph Strick, and starred Bosco Hogan as Stephen Dedalus.
35. Author interview with Keneally, January 17, 2020.
36. Kael, 1981.
37. Hall, 57.
38. Geraldine Pascall, *The Australian*, August 30, 1976.
39. Keith Connolly, *Herald Weekend*, August 7, 1976.
40. *Daily Telegraph*, May 31, 1976.
41. Kael, 1981.
42. Christos Tsiolkas, *The Devil's Playground* (Sydney: Currency Press;; and Canberra: ScreenSound Australia, 2002), 54.
43. Tsoilkas, *The Devil's Playground*, 64.
44. Tsoilkas, *The Devil's Playground*, 60.

CHAPTER THREE: A "MASTER-WORK"—*THE CHANT OF JIMMIE BLACKSMITH*

1. Pauline Kael, *Taking It All In: Film Writings, 1980–1983* (London: An Arena Book, 1987), 54.
2. Henry Reynolds, *The Chant of Jimmie Blacksmith* (Strawberry Hills, New South Wales: Australian Screen Classics, Currency Press, 2008), 4.
3. Author interview with Schepisi, August 2018.
4. Renee Ellis, "*Playboy* Interview: Fred Schepisi," July 1982, in Tom Ryan, ed., *Fred Schepisi: Interviews* (Jackson: University Press of Mississippi, 2017), 28.
5. Neil Rattigan, *Images of Australia* (Dallas: Southern Methodist University Press, 1991), 86.
6. Reynolds, 1.
7. Special feature on the thirtieth-anniversary DVD of *The Chant of Jimmie Blacksmith*, released of the film by Umbrella Aussie, 2008.
8. Reynolds, 16.
9. Reynolds, 62.
10. Reynolds, 70.
11. Brian McFarlane, *Words and Images: Australian Novels into Film* (Melbourne: Heinemann Publishers Australia and Cinema Papers, 1983), 89.

12. Thomas Keneally, *The Chant of Jimmie Blacksmith* (Sydney: A&R Classics, 2001 [1972]), 1. Other page references are to this edition.
13. Author interview with Keneally, January 17, 2020.
14. Rattigan, 87.
15. John Pym, *Monthly Film Bulletin* 46, no. 542 (March 1979): 40.
16. Pym, 41.
17. Baker in interview on the special features disc accompanying the thirtieth-anniversary DVD release of the film by Umbrella Aussie, 2008.
18. Schepisi.
19. Tom Ryan, in Ryan, ed., xiii.
20. Author interview with Keneally, January 17, 2020.
21. Reynolds, 34.
22. Reynolds, 61.
23. In Sue Mathews, *35mm Dreams: Conversations with Five Directors* (Ringwood, Victoria: Penguin Books, 1984), 42.

CHAPTER FOUR: MAKING IT OVERSEAS

1. Author interview with Fred Schepisi, Melbourne, August 2018.
2. Rennie Ellis, "*Playboy* Interview: Fred Schepisi," July 1982, in Tom Ryan, ed., *Fred Schepisi: Interviews* (Jackson: University Press of Mississippi, 2017), 31.
3. Vincent Canby, *Examiner*, September 11, 1982.
4. Janet Maslin, *New York Times*, July 25, 1982.
5. Ellis, 28
6. Reported in the *Australian National Times*, May 30, 1982.
7. Reported in the *Australian National Times*, May 30, 1982.
8. Barrie Pattison, *Cinema Papers*, Melbourne, December 1982, 567.
9. *Playboy* interview, in Ryan, ed., p.28.
10. Author interview with Schepisi, Melbourne, December 17, 2019.
11. Kevin Thomas, *Los Angeles Times*, October 23, 1982.
12. Keith Connelly, *Melbourne Herald*, September 23, 1982.
13. Helen Dalley, *The Bulletin*, May 11, 1982.
14. Schepisi interviewed in Sue Mathews, *35mm Dreams: Conversations with Five Directors* (Ringwood, Victoria: Penguin Books, 1984), 57.
15. Interview with Scott Murray, in Ryan, ed., 89.
16. Author interview with Schepisi, Melbourne, August 2018.
17. Janet Maslin, *New York Times*, July 25, 1984.
18. Michael Sragow, "Fred Schepisi: The Australian Director Talks about His New Controversial Film, *Barbarosa*," *Rolling Stone*, April 29, 1982, in Ryan, ed., 44.

19. Maslin, 1984.
20. Canby, *Examiner*, September 11, 1982.
21. Author interview with Schepisi, Melbourne, August 2018.
22. Roger Ebert, "*Iceman*, January 1 1984," in *Roger Ebert's Movie Home Companion* (Kansas City: Andrews and McMeel, 1990), 361.
23. Pauline Kael, *New Yorker*, April 30, 1984.
24. Quoted in James Verniere, "Fred Schepisi's *Iceman* Cometh: Altered States in the Great White North," *Film Comment*, September/October 1983, in Ryan, ed., 45.
25. Maslin, 1984.
26. Interview with David Edelstein, 1984, in Ryan, ed., 49.
27. Evan Williams, *Weekend Australian*, October 28–29, 1984.
28. Sandra Hall, *The Bulletin*, November 6, 1984.
29. Ivor Davies, *Australian Weekend Magazine*, April 28–29, 1984.
30. Verniere, in Ryan, ed., 46.
31. Ebert, 361–62.
32. https://www.imdb.com/title/tt0089816/?ref_=nm_flmg_dr_13.
33. *Monthly Film Bulletin* 52, no. 622 (November 1985): 344.
34. Julian Petley, "The Upright Houses & the Romantic Englishwoman," *Monthly Film Bulletin* 52, no. 614 (March 1985): 72.
35. In interview with David Stratton, "Man of Plenty," *Cinema Papers*, no. 56 (March 1986): 24.
36. Steve Lawson, "Hare Apparent," *Film Comment* 21, no. 5 (September–October 1985): 15.
37. Alex Pollak, *Sydney Morning Herald*, December 14, 1985.
38. Liz Smith, *San Francisco Chronicle*, September 231, 1985.
39. Judy Stone, "Director had *Plenty* to Say About the Film," *San Francisco Chronicle*, September 19, 1985.
40. Stratton interview.
41. "Dialogue on Film: Fred Schepisi," *American Film*, July–August 1987, 12.
42. Scott Murray, "Fred Schepisi: 'Pushing the Boundaries,'" in Ryan, ed., 92.
43. Stratton interview.
44. Pam Cook, *Monthly Film Bulletin* 52, no. 622 (November 1985): 345.
45. Stephen Schiff, "A Cinematic Gallant," *New Yorker*, December 20, 1993, in Ryan, ed., 103.
46. Vincent Canby, *New York Times*, September 19, 1985.
47. Charles Champlin, *Los Angeles Times*, September 28, 1985.
48. "Dialogue on Film: Fred Schepisi," *American Film*, July–August 1987, 12.
49. Judy Stone, *San Francisco Chronicle*, September 20, 1985.
50. Author interview with Schepisi, Melbourne, December 17, 2019.
51. Murray, in Ryan, ed., 95.

52. David Denby, *New Yorker*, June 15, 1987, 87.

53. Dan Callahan, "All Against One and One Against All: Fred Schepisi's Outsiders," *Sight & Sound*, February 5, 2014, https://www.bfi.org.uk/news-opinion/sight-sound-magazine/interviews/all-against-one-one-against-all-fred-schepisi-outsiders.

54. Author interview with Fred Schepisi, Melbourne, August 2018.

55. Ebert, 636.

56. Ebert, 636.

57. Murray, in Ryan, ed., 95.

58. Murray, in Ryan, ed., 97.

59. J. Hoberman, *Village Voice*, June 23, 1987.

60. Hal Hinson, "*Roxanne*," *Washington Post*, June 19, 1987.

61. Denby, 87.

62. Kim Newman, *Monthly Film Bulletin* 54, no. 646 (November 1987): 343.

CHAPTER FIVE: SCHEPISI AND THE CHAMBERLAIN AFFAIR— *A CRY IN THE DARK*

1. John Bryson, *Evil Angels* (Sydney, New South Wales: Hodder Headline Pty Ltd., 2000 [1985]).

2. Bryson, 540.

3. Bryson, 268.

4. Steve Brien, *Azaria: The Trial of the Century* (Australia: QB Books, 1984).

5. George W. Rollo, *The Azaria Mystery: A Reason to Kill* (Strathfield, New South Wales: G. W. Rollo, 1982).

6. Interview with Philippa Hawker, "The Making of Evil Angels," *Cinema Papers*, no. 70 (November 1988): 9.

7. Hawker, 9.

8. Author interview with Schepisi, Melbourne, August 2018.

9. David Stratton, *The Avocado Plantation* (Sydney: Pan Macmillan Publishers, 1991), 60.

10. Hawker, 68.

11. Hawker, 68.

12. Stratton, 60.

13. Author interview with Schepisi, Melbourne, August 2018.

14. Interview with Scott Murray, quoted in Tom Ryan, ed., *Fred Schepisi: Interviews* (Jackson: University Press of Mississippi, 2017), 96.

15. Bryson, 167.

16. Bryson, 119.

17. Interview with Peter Malone, quoted in Ryan, ed., 83.

18. Roger Ebert, "A Cry in the Dark," November 11, 1988, *Roger Ebert's Movie Home Companion* (Kansas City: Andrews and McMeel, 1990), 169.
19. Warwick McFadyen, "Pell Case Confronts Us with Workings of Justice," *The Age*, March 11, 2019.
20. Louise Sweet, "A Cry in the Dark," *Monthly Film Bulletin* 56, no. 665 (June 1989), 177.
21. Felicity Collins, "Evil Angels, *Cinema Papers*," no. 71 (January 1989), 71.
22. Interview with Hawker, 70.
23. Collins, 71.
24. Sweet, 178.
25. Ebert, 1988.
26. Paul LePetit, "Evil Angels," in Scott Hocking, ed., *100 Greatest Australian Films* (Richmond, Victoria: Scribal Publishing, 2000), 96.

CHAPTER SIX: AT HOME IN THE US

1. Interview with Scott Murray in Tom Ryan, ed., *Fred Schepisi: Interviews* (Jackson: University Press of Mississippi, 2017), 99.
2. Pathe Entertainment, Inc., production notes, 2.
3. Rennie Ellis, "The Man Meryl Streep Trusts," in Ryan, ed., 71.
4. Pathe Entertainment, Inc., production notes, 4.
5. Pathe Entertainment, Inc., production notes, 4.
6. Kim Newman, *Monthly Film Bulletin* 58, no. 686 (March 1991): 85.
7. Vincent Canby, "Sean Connery in *The Russia House*," *New York Times*, December 19, 1990, https://www.nytimes.com/1990/12/19/movies/review-film-sean-connery-in-the-russia-house.html.
8. Roger Ebert, "The Russia House," December 21, 1990, https://www.rogerebert.com/reviews/iq-1991.
9. Ingrid Jacobson, *Perth Sunday Times*, April 14, 1991.
10. Steven R. Weisman, *San Francisco Chronicle*, November 2, 1991.
11. Interview with Tom Ryan in Ryan, ed., 169.
12. Ryan, 170.
13. Janet Maslin, *New York Times*, October 2, 1992.
14. Mick LaSalle, *San Francisco Chronicle*, October 2, 1992.
15. Roger Ebert, "Mr. Baseball," October 2, 1992, https://www.rogerebert.com/reviews/mr-baseball-1992.
16. Hal Hinson, *Washington Post*, October 2, 1992.
17. Gordon E. Slethaug, *Adaptation Theory and Criticism* (New York: Bloomsbury, 2014), 35, 36.
18. Slethaug, 36.

19. Interview with author, Melbourne, August 2018.

20. John Guare quoted in Stephen Schiff, "A Cinematic Gallant," *New Yorker*, December 20, 1993, in Ryan, ed., 104.

21. Slethaug, 47.

22. Slethaug, 47, Schepisi quoted.

23. John Guare, *Six Degrees of Separation* (New York: Vintage Books, second edition, 1994 [1990]), 4.

24. Guare, 31–33. For example, Paul's three-page speech about *The Catcher in the Rye*.

25. Interview with Ryan, in Ryan, ed., 165.

26. Brian McFarlane, "*Six Degrees of Separation*," *Cinema Papers*, June 1995, 48.

27. Interview with Ryan, in Ryan, ed., 169.

28. Author interview with Jill Bilcock, Melbourne, April 11, 2019.

29. Rita Kempley, *Washington Post*, December 22, 1933, http://www.washingtonpost.com/wp-srv/style/longterm/movies/videos/sixdegreesofseparationrkempley_a0a3dd.htm.

30. Geoffrey Macnab, *Sight and Sound* 5, no. 7 (July 1995): 54.

31. Quoted in the film's production notes, 3

32. J. Hoberman, *Village Voice*, January 3, 1995,

33. Mark Naglazas, *West Australian*, May 11, 1995.

34. Production notes, 4.

35. Roger Ebert, "*I.Q.*," December 24, 1994, https://www.rogerebert.com/reviews/iq-1994.

36. Keith Bailey, "The Unknown Movies: *I.Q.*," May 30, 2015, http://www.the-unknown-movies.com/unknownmovies/reviews/rev672.html.

37. Hal Hinson, "*I.Q.*," December 25, 1994, http://www.washingtonpost.com/wp-srv/style/longterm/movies/videos/iqpghinson_a0bd9c.htm.

38. Chris Darke, *Sight and Sound*, March 1995, 42.

39. Janet Maslin, *New York Times*, December 23, 1994.

40. Hal Hinson, *Washington Post*, December 25, 1994.

41. Barbara Creed, *The Age*, May 11, 1995.

42. Naglazas, *West Australian*, May 11, 1995.

43. Interview with Ryan, in Ryan, ed., 168.

44. Interview with author, Melbourne, August 2018.

45. Interview with Ryan, in Ryan, ed., 174.

46. Ryan, in Ryan, ed., xv.

47. Dan Callahan, "All Against One and One Against All: Fred Schepisi's Outsiders," *Sight & Sound*, https://www.bfi.org.uk/news-opinion/sight-sound-magazine/interviews/all-against-one-one-against-all-fred-schepisi-outsiders.

48. Leslie Felperin, *Sight & Sound* 7, no. 3 (March 1997): 47.

CHAPTER SEVEN: TRIUMPH IN THE UK—*LAST ORDERS* (2002)

1. Graham Swift, *Last Orders* (London: Picador, 2010 [1996]).
2. Interview with author, Melbourne, August 2018.
3. Interview with author, Melbourne, August 2018.
4. Brian Tufano in interview with author, England, October 2019.
5. Brian McFarlane, "The Sense of an Adaptation," *Inside Story*, May 25, 2017, https://insidestory.org.au/the-sense-of-an-adaptation/.
6. Ryan Gilbey, "Unmade Freds," *Sight & Sound* 12, no. 1 (January 2002): 12.
7. Cynthia Fuchs, "*Last Orders*: An Interview with Director Fred Schepisi," December 7, 2001, in Tom Ryan, ed., *Fred Schepisi Interviews* (Jackson: University Press of Mississippi, 2017), 114.
8. Quoted in Tom Ryan, "Fred Schepisi on *Last Orders*," in Ryan, ed., 124.
9. Swift, 222.
10. Roger Ebert, https://www.rogerebert.com/reviews/last-orders-2002.
11. Swift, *Last Orders* (London: Picador, 1996), 288.
12. A.O. Scott, *New York Times*, February 15, 2002.
13. Richard Falcon, *Sight and Sound* 12, no. 1: 49.
14. Mick LaSalle and Edward Guthmann, *San Francisco Chronicle*, March 1, 2002, https://www.sfgate.com/movies/article/FILM-CLIPS-Also-opening-today-2868346.php.
15. Peter Travers, *Rolling Stone*, February 13, 2002, https://www.rollingstone.com/movies/movie-reviews/last-orders-249621/.

CHAPTER EIGHT: IN THE NEW CENTURY

1. Stephen Holden, "Film Review: Fathers, Sons, Grandsons, In the Script and Real Life," *New York Times*, April 25, 2003, https://www.nytimes.com/2003/04/25/movies/film-review-fathers-sons-grandsons-in-the-script-and-real-life.html.
2. Paul Le Petit, *New South Wales Sunday Telegraph*, August 31, 2003.
3. "Fred Schepisi on *It Runs in the Family*, in Tom Ryan, ed., *Fred Schepisi: Interviews* (Jackson: University Press of Mississippi, 2017), 127–37.
4. Production notes, 14
5. Production notes, 11.
6. Schepisi, in Ryan, ed., 129.
7. Schepisi, in Ryan, ed., 129.
8. Jamie Russell, "*It Runs in the Family*," BBC Films, http://www.bbc.co.uk/films/2003/09/02/it_runs_in_the_family_2003_review.shtml.
9. Schepisi, in Ryan, 131.

10. Roger Ebert, https://www.rogerebert.com/reviews/it-runs-in-the-family-2003.
11. Holden, 2003.
12. Ebert, 2003.
13. Ali Jaafar, *Sight & Sound* 13, no. 11 (November 2003): 50.
14. Holden, 2003.
15. Ebert, 2003.
16. Holden, 2003.
17. Mick LaSalle, "It Runs in the Family," https://www.sfgate.com/movies/article/FILM-CLIPS-Also-opening-today-2652881.php.
18. Russell, 2003.
19. Jaafar, 50.
20. Reviews in *Urban Cinefile*, August 2003, http://www.urbancinefile.com.au/home/view.asp?a=7753&s=Reviews.
21. Leigh Paatsch, *(Melbourne) Herald Sun*, August, 21 2003.
22. Richard Russo, *Empire Falls* (London: Vintage Books, Random House, 2001). All references to the book are from this edition.
23. Schepisi, in Ryan, 175.
24. Author interview with Schepisi, Melbourne, August 2018.
25. Schepisi, in Ryan, ed., 175.
26. Audio commentary on DVD, HBO Films, 2006.
27. Russo, 12.
28. Ted Gioia, http://www.thenewcanon.com/empire_falls.html.
29. Glenn Erickson, *DVD Talk*, https://www.dvdtalk.com/dvdsavant/s1736fall.html
30. DVD.
31. Brian Lowry, *Variety*, May 25, 2005, https://variety.com/2005/tv/reviews/empire-falls-1200525541/.
32. John Leonard, *New York*, May 18, 2005, http://nymag.com/nymetro/arts/tv/reviews/12036/.
33. Jon Cvack, https://www.yellowbarrel.org/films/empire-falls-2005-part-2-of-22019.

CHAPTER NINE: AT HOME AND ABROAD

1. Tom Ryan, "Fred Schepisi on Making Movies," in Ryan, ed., *Fred Schepisi: Interviews* (Jackson: University Press of Mississippi, 2017), 135.
2. David Marr, *Patrick White—A Life* (Sydney: Random House Australia, 1991), 494.
3. Patrick White, *The Eye of the Storm* (Harmondsworth, UK: Penguin, 1975 [1973]), 12. All references are from this edition.

NOTES

4. In conversation with Courtney Dawson, "On Screen," *Canberra Times*, September 15, 2011, 7.
5. Michael Bodey, "Right said Fred," *The Australian*, September 10, 2011.
6. Sandra Hall, *Sydney Morning Herald*, September 15, 2011, 16.
7. Schepisi, in Ryan, ed., 153.
8. The setting was in fact the historic Melbourne mansion in Ripponlea, Melbourne.
9. Marr, 512.
10. Marr, 513.
11. Author interview with Helen Morse, Melbourne, September 19, 2019.
12. Author interview with Helen Morse, Melbourne, September 19, 2019.
13. David Melville, *Senses of Cinema*, no. 70 (February 2014), http://sensesof cinema.com/2014/key-moments-in-australian-cinema-issue-70-march-2014 /the-death-of-venus-inside-the-eye-of-the-storm-fred-schepisi-2011/
14. White, 589.
15. Author interview with Ian Baker, Melbourne, April 2019.
16. The poem, by Georg Trakl, and the words for "Tingeltangel" were originally by Patrick White.
17. Author interview with Helen Morse.
18. Don Groves, SBS World Movies, https://www.sbs.com.au/movies/review /eye-storm-review.
19. Megan Lehmann, https://www.hollywoodreporter.com/review/eye-storm -film-review-214479.
20. Nick Schager, https://www.villagevoice.com/2012/09/05/the-eye-of-the -storm-film-review/.
21. Interview produced by David E Van Houten on the special features on the Umbrella Entertainment DVD of *Eye of the Storm*.
22. Michael Bodey, *The Australian*, July 16, 2014.
23. Schepisi quoted in Bodey.
24. Information given on the Internet Movie Database.
25. Internet Movie Database. Also, the film was not reviewed in *Sight & Sound*, which reviews all new features released in the UK.
26. Interview with author, Melbourne, December 17, 2019.
27. Van Houten, DVD interview.
28. Michael Dequina, http://1moviereport.com/movierpt2014–05b.html#words.
29. Eddie Cockrell, *Weekend Australian*, July 19, 2014.
30. Van Houten, DVD interview.
31. Ed Gibbs, https://www.sbs.com.au/movies/review/words-and-pictures-review.
32. Author interview with Ian Baker.
33. Cockrell, 2014.

34. Quoted in Esther Levy-Fenner, "Painting with Words and Pictures," *Arts Hub*, July 8, 2014, https://www.artshub.com.au/news-article/sponsored-content/film/esther-levy-fenner/painting-with-words-and-pictures-244558.

CONCLUSION

1. Author interview with Schepisi, Melbourne, December 17, 2019.
2. Author interview with Schepisi, Melbourne, December 17, 2019.
3. Brian McFarlane and Geoff Mayer, *New Australian Cinema: Sources and Parallels in American and British Films* (Cambridge and Melbourne: Cambridge University Press, 1992).
4. Tom O' Regan, *Australian National Cinema* (London and New York: Routledge, 1996), 238.
5. In title of interview with Tom Ryan, in Ryan, ed., *Fred Schepisi: Interviews* (Jackson: University Press of Mississippi, 2017), 153.
6. Author interview with Schepisi, August 2018.

SELECT BIBLIOGRAPHY

The following lists the books and extended articles referred to in the chapters of this study. Details of individual reviews and interviews in journals and newspapers are given in the endnotes following relevant chapter.

Bryson, John. *Evil Angels.* Sydney Hodder Headline Pty Ltd., 2000 (1985).
Dermody, Susan, and Elizabeth Jacka. *The Screening of Australia*, volumes 1 and 2. Sydney: Currency Press, 1987, 1988.
Ebert, Roger. *Roger Ebert's Movie Home Companion.* Kansas City: Andrews and McMeel, 1990.
Gilbey, Ryan. "Unmade Freds." *Sight & Sound* 12, no. 1 (January 2002).
Guare, John. *Six Degrees of Separation.* New York: Vintage Books, second edition, 1994.
Hall, Sandra. *Critical Business: The New Australian Cinema in Review.* In Adelaide et al.: Rigby, 1985.
Kael, Pauline. *Taking It All In: Film Writings, 1980–1983.* London: An Arena Book, 1987.
Keneally, Thomas. *The Chant of Jimmie Blacksmith.* Sydney: A&R Classics, 2001 (1972).
LePetit, Paul. "*Evil Angels.*" In Scott Hocking, ed., *100 Greatest Australian Films.* Richmond, Victoria: Scribal Publishing, 2000.
Malone, Peter, ed. *Myth & Meaning: Australian Film Directors in their Own Words.* Sydney: Currency Press, 2001.
Malone, Peter, ed. *Through a Catholic Lens: Religious Perspectives of Nineteen Film Directors from Around the World.* Lanham, MD: Rowman & Littlefield, 2007.
Marr, David. *Patrick White—A Life.* Sydney: Random House Australia, 1991.
Matthews, Sue, ed. *35mm Dreams: Conversations with Five Directors.* Ringwood, Victoria: Penguin Books, 1984.
McFarlane, Brian. *Words and Images: Australian Novels into Film.* Richmond, Victoria: Heinemann Publishers Australia, 1983.

McFarlane, Brian, and Geoff Mayer. *New Australian Cinema: Sources and Parallels in American and British Film.* Oakleigh, Victoria: Cambridge University Press, 1992.

Moran, Albert, and Tom O'Regan, eds. *An Australian Film Reader.* Sydney: Currency Press, 1985.

Moran, Albert, and Tom O'Regan, eds. *The Australian Screen.* Ringwood, Victoria: Penguin Books, 1989.

Morris, Meaghan. "Personal Relationships and Sexuality." In Scott Murray, ed., *New Australian Cinema.* Melbourne: Thomas Nelson, 1980.

Murray, John B. "The Guild—A Brief History," essay accompanying the DVD released by Guild Productions Pty Ltd. N.d.

Murray, Scott, ed. *Australian Cinema.* St. Leonard's, New South Wales: Allen & Unwin, with Australian Film Commission, 1994.

Murray, Scott, ed. *Australian Film, 1978–1994.* Melbourne: Oxford University Press, 1995.

Murray, Scott, ed. *New Australian Cinema.* Melbourne: Thomas Nelson, 1980.

O'Regan, Tom. *Australian National Cinema.* London and New York: Routledge, 1996.

Pike, Andrew, and Ross Cooper. *Australian Film, 1900–1977.* Melbourne: Oxford University Press, 1980, revised edition 1998.

Rattigan, Neil. *Images of Australia.* Dallas: Southern Methodist University Press, 1991.

Reynolds, Henry. *The Chant of Jimmie Blacksmith.* Sydney: Currency Press, Australian Screen Classics, 2008.

Russo, Richard. *Empire Falls.* London: Vintage Books, Random House, 2001.

Ryan, Tom, ed. *Fred Schepisi: Interviews.* Jackson: University Press of Mississippi, 2017.

Shirley, Graham, and Brian Adams. *Australian Cinema: The First Eighty Years.* Australia: Angus & Robertson Publishers and Currency Press, 1983.

Slethaug, Gordon E. *Adaptation Theory and Criticism.* New York: Bloomsbury, 2014.

Stratton, David. *The Avocado Plantation.* Sydney: Pan Macmillan Publishers, 1990.

Swift, Graham. *Last Orders.* London: Picador, 2010 (1996).

Tsiolkas, Christos. *The Devil's Playground.* Sydney: Currency Press, 2002.

White, Patrick. *The Eye of the Storm.* Harmondsworth, UK: Penguin, 1973 (1975).

INDEX

Adams, Philip, 5
adaptation, 31, 33, 52, 74, 85, 89, 99, 100, 138
Adventures of Barry McKenzie, The, 11, 16
Alexander, Elizabeth, 35
Alfie, 109
Alvin Purple, 11, 16
Anderson, Brian, 37
Anderson, Gillian, 147
Anderson, Lindsay, 7
Andorra, 147
Antonioni, Michelangelo, 109
Archer, Jillian, 23
Armstrong, Gillian, 3, 4, 27, 29, 42, 146
Australian cinema revival, 3, 11, 17, 27, 29, 31, 42, 139
Australian Film Commission, 18, 69
Australian Film Institute, 7
Australian Film Studios, Dallas, 69
Ayers Rock, 70, 72

Babe: Pig in the City, 133
Baker, Ian, 9, 13, 15, 18, 19, 32, 34, 36, 42, 46, 48, 54, 55, 58, 62, 72, 74, 79, 89, 90, 91, 115, 122, 126, 133, 138, 144, 145
Ball of Fire, 92
Barbarosa, 19, 42, 43–47, 51, 61, 82, 89, 97, 148
Barnes, Julian, 100
Barrett, Ray, 34
Batra, Ritesh, 100

Bells of St Mary's, The, 15
Beresford, Bruce, 3, 4, 27, 29, 42, 57, 146
Bilcock, Jill, 71, 72, 74, 90, 93
Billy Liar!, 109
Binoche, Juliette, 141, 142, 143, 144
Blow-Up, 109
Boer War, 32
Brandauer, Klaus Maria, 79
Brandenstein, Patrizia von, 90, 115, 144, 145
Breckman, Andy, 93
British "New Wave" films, 97, 109
Bryson, John, 66, 67–69, 70, 73, 76
Burke, Simon, 19
Burstall, Tim, 12
Burton, Kate, 128
Busey, Gary, 44, 46

Caine, Michael, 101, 108, 109, 110
Callahan, Dan, 96
Canby, Vincent, 43, 47, 59, 80
Cannes Film Festival, 26, 28
Can't You Hear Me Callin', Caroline, 9
Canterbury Cathedral, 105, 141
Carden Advertising, 5
Carroll, Peter, 38, 39
Caswell, Robert, 69, 70, 74
Chains, 84
Chamberlain, Lindy, 66, 70, 74
Chamberlain, Michael, 66, 67, 69, 73, 74
Chamberlain affair, 66–67, 73–74
Chandler, Miles, 123

INDEX

Channing, Stockard, 87, 89–90, 125
Chant of Jimmie Blacksmith, The (film), ix, 17, 28–41, 42, 43, 45, 46, 47–48, 52, 58, 61, 75, 78, 82, 146, 148, 149
Chant of Jimmie Blacksmith, The (novel), 28–32, 68, 120
Chatham Naval War Memorial, 103
Choudhury, Sarita, 115
Cimino, Michael, 43
Cinema Papers, ix
Cinema Verity, 69
Cinesound, 5, 6
Cleese, John, 95, 96
Cole, Stephen, 108
comedy, 60, 63, 64, 95, 143–44
Commonwealth Film Unit, 8
Connery, Sean, 78, 80, 81, 95, 149
Courtenay, Tom, 101, 108, 109–10
Cox, Peter, 23
Cracknell, Ruth, 35
Creed, Barbara, 95
Crichton, Charles, 96
Crosby, Don, 35
Crouse, Lindsay, 49, 51
Cry in the Dark, A, 60, 66–76, 77, 78, 82, 86, 90, 141, 148, 149
Culkin, Rory, 114
Curtis, Jamie Lee, 96
Cyrano de Bergerac, 61

Dance, Charles, 56
Darin, Bobby, 116
Davis, Judy, 134, 137, 138
Davison, Bruce, 88
Dawson, Julie, 34
De La Paz, Danny, 44
Denby, David, 60, 64
Depardieu, Gérard, 61
Devil's Playground, The, ix, 3, 4, 16, 17–27, 28, 42, 58, 60, 123, 148
Diamonds Are Forever, 80

Diedrich, John, 25
Dignam, Arthur, 13, 14, 16, 18, 19, 22, 23, 37
Di Pego, Gerald, 142, 143
Doring, Melinda, 138
Douglas, Cameron, 112, 113, 114, 117
Douglas, Diana, 112, 113, 115
Douglas, Kirk, 112, 113, 114, 117
Douglas, Michael, 112, 113, 114, 117
Drimmer, John, 49
Duggan, Gerry, 24

Ebert, Roger, 47, 51, 61, 64, 72, 76, 81, 84, 94, 106, 117, 118, 119
Einstein, Albert, 91–92, 94
Ellis, Bob, 16
Ellis, Rennie, 44
Empire Falls (film), 112, 120–30, 133, 148, 149, 150
Empire Falls (novel), 120, 121, 122, 123, 130, 133, 146, 149
Every Day Except Christmas, 7
Evil Angels (book). *See* Bryson, John
Evil Angels (film). *See Cry in the Dark, A*
Eye of the Storm, The (film), ix, 61, 112, 130–39, 147, 149
Eye of the Storm, The (novel), 112, 120, 131, 133, 147

Farina, Dennis, 123
Federation, 8, 29, 32, 34, 39, 52, 148
Feild, JJ, 108
Ferrer, José, 61
Fierce Creatures, 95–96
Film House, 5, 7, 9, 13, 18, 42
Finlayson, Rhonda, 14
Fish Called Wanda, A, 96
Fitchner, Michael, 126
Ford, John, 39, 43, 45
Fox, James, 78, 79
Fred Schepisi: Interviews (2017), x

INDEX

French Lieutenant's Woman, The, 55
Friels, Colin, 136, 138
Fry, Stephen, 92

Gaden, John, 135, 138
Gascone, Nicholas, 83
G.B.H., 96
Getting of Wisdom, 4, 29
Gielgud, Sir John, 24, 55, 56
Going My Way, 23
Golan-Globus Production, 69
Goldsmith, Jerry, 90, 92
Gordon, Michael, 61
Gorovala, Irina, 115
Governor, Jimmy, 29–31
Grabowsky, Paul, 114, 122, 138, 141
Gray, Vivean, 14
Greater Union Organisation, 16
Greenwood, Bruce, 144
Griffin, Walter Burleigh, 8
Guare, John, 84, 85, 86, 87, 89, 121, 133

Hall, Anthony Michael, 89
Hall, Sandra, 16, 133
Hammer, Mark, 115, 117
Hampton, David, 85
Hannah, Daryl, 62, 64
Harders, Jane, 34
Hare, Sir David, 52–53, 57, 121
Harris, Ed, 123, 124, 125, 128, 129, 149
Hart, Kitty Carlisle, 88
Hawks, Howard, 43
Helland, J. Roy, 58
Hellier, Trudy, 136
Heaven's Gate, 43
Hemmings, David, 100, 108, 109
Hemmings, Nolan, 108
Hill in Korea, A, 109
Hinson, Hal, 95
Hoberman, J., 92
Hoffman, Philip Seymour, 126

Holden, Stephen, 117, 118
Honess, Peter, 83, 87, 90, 102, 145
Hoskins, Bob, 100, 108, 110
Houghton, Peter, 136
Hunt, Helen, 123
Hunter, Jeffrey, 45
Hurst, Sally, 103
Hurt, Mary Beth, 88
Hutton, Tim, 49, 51
Honeysuckle Rose, 45
Hundred-Odd Years from Now, A, 7–8

Iceman, 47–51, 60, 61, 82
Idle, Eric, 96
Innes, George, 101
I.Q., 77, 90, 91–95, 144
It Runs in the Family, 112–20, 122, 125, 150

Jack and Jill: A Postscript, 11
Jacobi, Lou, 92
Joyce, James, 24
Junkerman, John, 82

Kael, Pauline, 24, 25, 26, 28, 43, 49
Karinthy, Frigyes, 84
Kavanagh, Brian, 6, 7, 13, 36
Katz, Gene, 92
Keller, Louise, 119
Keneally, Thomas, 11, 13, 16, 18, 24, 28, 29–32, 41
Klimov, Elem, 77
Kline, Kevin, 96
Kramer vs. Kramer, 58

Ladd, Alan, Jr., 77
Lambert, Verity, 66, 68
Lassally, Walter, 7
Last Orders, ix, 61, 82, 97–111, 113, 121, 125, 126, 141, 146, 150
Le Carré, John, 77, 78, 79, 81
Leeson, Michael, 93

Leigh, Mike, 97
Leonard, John, 130
Lewis, Tommy, 30, 33, 36
Libido, 9, 10, 12–13, 15, 16, 18, 28; *The Child*, 12; *The Family Man*, 12; *The Husband*, 12; *The Priest*, 10, 12, 18
Loach, Ken, 97
Lone, John, 49, 51
Loneliness of the Long-Distance Runner, The, 109
Long Good Friday, The, 110
Losey, Joseph, 132
Lowell, Carey, 28

MacDonald, Richard, 58
Malone, Peter, 20
Manhattan, 114, 141
Margate Pier, 98, 101, 103, 105–6
Marr, David, 131–32, 134
Martin, Steve, 60, 62, 64, 82
Maslin, Janet, 43, 46, 47, 50, 82, 95
Masur, Richard, 88
Matsushita Electric Industrial Co., 81, 82
Matthau, Walter, 91, 93–94, 95
Matthews, Sue, 4, 5
Mayer, Joseph, 92
McCallum, Charles, 19
McGregor, Craig, 11
McKellen, Sir Ian, 55, 59, 87
Mercer, David, 132
Merrick, Monte, 82
Metro, ix
Mirren, Dame Helen, 102, 108, 111
Monaghan, Michelle, 115
Morris, Judy, 132, 133, 134, 147
Morris, Meaghan, 11, 14
Morse, Helen, 135, 138
Mr. Baseball, 77, 81–84
Murray, John B., 10, 12, 13
My Brilliant Career, 4, 29
Myers, Ruth, 58

Naked Bunyip, The, 11
Negahban, Navid, 142
Neill, Sam, 55, 69, 75
Nelligan, Kate, 54
Nelson, Willy, 44, 45, 46
Nevin, Robyn, 13, 14, 15, 38, 136, 138
Newman, Kim, 64
Newman, Paul, 120, 123
Night the Prowler, The, 132
Nil by Mouth, 110
Nobel Prize for Literature, 131
Noyce, Philip, 42

"ocker" comedies, 11, 12
On Golden Pond, 119
Onward Speed, 9
outsiders, 33–35, 44, 75, 86
Owen, Clive, 141, 142, 143, 144, 147

Palin, Michael, 96
Panabaker, Danielle, 125
Papp, Joe, 54
Parsons, Estelle, 123
Party, 9
Paton Advertising Service, 5
Pelletier, Theo, 82
Penn, Robin Wright, 123
People Make Papers, 6–7
Peters, Bernadette, 114, 116
Pfeiffer, Michelle, 79, 80, 81, 95
Phelan, Anne, 23
Picnic at Hanging Rock, 4, 29
Pine, Larry, 122
Plenty, ix, 51–59, 60, 61, 68, 69, 76, 77, 78, 120, 121, 141
Porter, Hal, 11
Portrait of the Artist as a Young Man, A, 24
Press for Time, 111
Pressman, Edward R., 52, 54
Priest, The, 10, 12, 18

INDEX 179

Producers and Directors Guild of Australia, 10, 13
Proser, Chris, 49
Punch, Angela, 35

Quartet, 110
Quinn, Aidan, 125

Rampling, Charlotte, 133, 138, 149
Rappeneau, Jean-Paul, 61
Rattigan, Neil, 20, 21, 29, 34
realism, 15, 29, 54, 97, 98
Redgrave, Vanessa, 147
Reisz, Karel, 55
Reynolds, Freddy, 35
Reynolds, Henry, 30–31, 40
Robbins, Tim, 92, 94–95
Robertson, Tim, 34
Roland, Gilbert, 44, 46
Ross, Gary, 82
Rossovich, Rick, 60, 64
Rostand, Edmond, 61, 62
Roxanne, 60–65, 68, 77, 82, 85, 89, 120, 122, 139, 140, 144, 148, 149
Rush, Geoffrey, 135, 136–37, 138
Russell, Ken, 80
Russia House, The, 77–81, 95, 149
Russo, Richard, 120, 121, 123, 129, 130, 133
Ryan, Meg, 92, 94–95
Ryan, Terry, 138
Ryan, Tom, x, 113

Scheider, Roy, 78, 79
Schepisi, Alexandra, 135
Schepisi, Fred: adaptability, x, 77, 148, 149; adaptation, x, 31, 52, 53, 61, 74, 84, 85–86, 89, 98–99, 100, 120, 133, 136, 149; advertising, 4–5, 18; Australian film revival, 3, 4, 11, 17, 27, 29, 31, 40, 42; autobiographical sources, 17; awards, 4, 5, 7, 18, 28; biographical elements, 3, 4, 17; box-office responses, 16, 26, 40–41, 64, 144; business sense, x, 3, 5, 18, 42, 46; Catholic background, 3, 16, 17, 18, 20, 23, 25; collaborators, 9, 13, 18, 36, 42, 52, 58, 74, 89, 90–91, 143, 149; coming-of-age theme, 4, 17, 37; cultural change, 11, 12, 29, 52; documentaries, 5, 6–9; education, 3; environments, 9, 17, 19, 29, 37, 44, 48, 51, 82, 145, 146; genres, x, 43, 45, 47, 60, 77; finance, 10, 40, 43, 54, 140; humane approach, 131, 132; location filming, 46–47, 49, 51, 56, 61, 69, 79, 91, 115; political contexts, 4, 38, 56, 58; short films, 4, 6–9, 13; television experience, 3, 4, 5, 112, 120, 129; thematic interests, x, 4, 33, 43–44, 47; UK experience, 3, 5, 52, 55, 60; unmade projects, 147; US experience, 3, 42, 46, 52, 55, 60, 77; visual qualities, x, 9, 19, 21, 33, 40, 59, 61, 71, 72, 100, 107, 137, 138
Schneider, Christian, 144
science-fiction, 47–51, 148
screwball comedies, 92
Searchers, The, 39, 45, 46
Selleck, Tom, 82, 83, 84
Sense of an Ending, The, 100
Senses of Cinema, ix
Shape of Quality, The, 6
Sharman, Jim, 132
Six Degrees of Separation (film), ix, 61, 77, 78, 82, 84–91, 97, 107, 112, 114, 115, 120, 121, 146, 122, 123, 125, 141, 148, 149, 150
Six Degrees of Separation (play), 85, 86, 89, 133
Slethaug, Gordon E., 86
Smeaton, Bruce, 13, 18, 19, 27, 42, 48, 54, 55
Smith, Will, 87, 90, 148
Sophie's Choice, 58

Soviet Filmmakers Union, 77
Splitting Heirs, 96
Sting, 57
Stitt, Alex, 5
Stoppard, Sir Tom, 77, 79, 121
Stork, 11
Stratton, David, 69
Streep, Meryl, 52, 53, 54–55, 58, 68, 69, 75
Suez crisis, 58, 59
Sutherland, Donald, 87
Swift, Graham, 98, 99, 100, 101, 103, 111, 121

Takakura, Ken, 84
Takanashi, Ava, 83
Tate, Nick, 23
Tesich, Steve, 60
Theodorakis, Maria, 135
Thomas, Max, 16
Thompson, Jack, 33
Tien, Valerie, 144
Tomorrow's Canberra, 8–9
Tsiolkas, Christos, 26–27
Tufano, Brian, 100, 102, 103, 106
Twenty British Films: A Guided Tour, ix

Ullman, Tracey, 57
Uluru, 66, 72
Universal, 43, 81
Urban, Andrew L., 119

Veysey, Kristen, 134
Vikings, The, 117
von Brandenstein, Patrizia. *See* Brandenstein, Patrizia von
Voss, 132

Wade, Kevin, 82
War Zone, 110
Wayne, John, 45
Weatherhead, Bruce, 5
Weir, Peter, 3, 4, 27, 29, 42, 57, 146
Westerns, 43, 45, 47
Wetherby, 52
White, Patrick, 131, 132, 133, 134, 139
Whitlam, Gough, 4
Wigutow, Jesse, 113, 116, 118
Williams, Cheryl, 134
Williams, Evan, 50
Williams, Kate, 138, 139
Williamson, David, 11
Winstone, Ray, 101, 108, 110
Winterbottom, Michael, 97
Wisdom, Norman, 111
Wittliff, William, 44, 45
Woodward, Joanne, 123, 124, 128
Words and Images, ix
Words and Pictures, 139–45
Wurzel, Stuart, 122

Young, Robert, 96

ABOUT THE AUTHOR

Photo Courtesy of the author

Brian McFarlane is adjunct associate professor in the Department of English at Monash University and adjunct professor in the Faculty of Health, Arts, and Design at Swinburne University of Technology. He is author or editor of several books, including *The Encyclopedia of British Film*.

OTHER BOOKS BY BRIAN McFARLANE

The Never-Ending. Brief Encounter, Manchester University Press, 2019.
Four from the Forties: Arliss, Crabtree, Knowles and Huntington. Manchester University Press, 2018.
Making a Meal of It: Writing about Film. Monash University Publishing, 2018.
Class-Act: The Lives and Careers of Googie Withers and John McCallum. Monash University Publishing, 2015.

Twenty British Films: A Guided Tour. Manchester University Press, 2015.
The Encyclopedia of British Film, fourth edition. Manchester University Press, 2014.
Real and Reel: The Education of a Film Obsessive and Critic. Sid Harta Publishers, 2010.
Michael Winterbottom (with Deane Williams). British Film Makers series, Manchester University Press, 2009.
The British "B" Film (with Steve Chibnall). British Film Institute, 2009.
Screen Adaptations: Charles Dickens' Great Expectations. Methuen Drama, 2008.
The Cinema of Britain and Ireland (ed.). Wallflower Press, 2005.
The Encyclopedia of British Film. Methuen, 2003.
Lance Comfort (British Film Makers). Manchester University Press, 2000.
The Oxford Companion to Australian Film (with Geoff Mayer and Ina Bertrand). Oxford University Press, 1999.
An Autobiography of British Cinema. Methuen Publishing Ltd., 1997.
Novel to Film: An Introduction to the Theory of Adaptation. Clarendon Press, Oxford, 1996.
Sixty Voices: Celebrities Recall the Golden Age of British Cinema. British Film Institute, 1993.
New Australian Cinema: Sources and Parallels in American and British Film (with Geoff Mayer). Cambridge University Press, 1992.
Viewpoints on Film (ed.). Longman Cheshire, 1992.
Viewpoints on the Nineteenth-Century Novel (ed.). Longman Cheshire, 1992.
Australian Cinema, 1970–1985. William Heinemann Australia, 1988.
Cross-Country: A Book of Australian Verse (with John Barnes). Heinemann Educational Australia, 1988.
Words and Images: Australian Novels into Film. Heinemann Publishers Australia, 1983.
Martin Boyd's "Langton Novels." Edward Arnold, 1980.

Printed in the United States
by Baker & Taylor Publisher Services